RESCUING
HOPE

A MEMOIR OF KAYLA BONAR

SONYA BONAR

Rescuing Hope:
A Memoir of Kayla Bonar

© 2022 Sonya Bonar

ISBN 978-0-578-28974-8

Purple Ink Publishing
Shohomish, Washington
purple.ink.publishing.2021@gmail.com

Printed in the United States of America

IN LOVING MEMORY

Kayla Nicole Bonar
February 10, 1995 – December 6, 2018

Rescuing HOPE

a memoir

by Kayla Bonar

Acknowledgements

I want to thank my family members who encouraged me to share our story using Kayla's blog. "You should write a book" was a phrase I heard more than once.

I want to thank my husband, Brian, for supporting me by giving me the time and space I needed. "You're the best."

Thank you to each one of my children, whom I love deeply. I pray that you can get to know Kayla's heart better through this book, especially those of you who were too young to know her well.

Thank you to my parents for teaching me to work hard, to love the Lord, and to be grateful.

Thank you to Peggy Rubenzer for your time and excellent talents to read and make many edits. I am deeply grateful.

Most of all, thank you to my Heavenly Father for sustaining me through this trial of loss. Thank you for sacrificing Your life on the cross so that I may live eternally with You.

Preface

"Inside every human being is a story waiting to be told. 'Rescuing Hope' is a book about hurt, hope, and healing; but mainly hope. It's also a story about love and laughter and the beautiful people I've met thus far by sharing my own brokenness. In sharing my words with others, hoping that someone reading them would understand, I found empathy. I traded self-pity for empathy and my life has been better ever since.

My desire is that after reading my book you'd find hope and healing in your life, or encourage another seeking those things in their own life. These words aren't meant to persuade you to chase after a better life the same way I did. On the contrary, I deeply desire that you'd find clarity regarding the platform on which you practically apply the gift that is empathy.

During my years as a college student, I began noticing that my testimony resonated with my friends, family, classmates, and professors. I discovered that vulnerability was immensely infectious. The various communities I was involved with and surrounded with began to feel compelled to share their stories with me. I've learned that there is power within a single story to influence and inspire the birth of many, many others. But it always starts with one. And it's up to you and me to decide if we'll step up to the plate and be the first."
(Kayla-2018)

When cleaning out Kayla's apartment, I found a notebook that she had started titled "My Memoir." This was the first page she wrote, so when I decided to attempt writing my story, I thought, "This will be the preface." Well, almost two years after finding this, here I am, attempting to share my story with a desire to bring hope.

Her desire, and mine, is to share our personal stories to incline others to tell theirs. When I meet someone new, I always look forward to hearing about their trials, joys, accomplishments, and hopes.

My hope for Kayla was always a life lived well, and a life with purpose. In her short 23 years, I believe, by the grace of God, she and He accomplished that together. I feel so humbled to be able to tell her story through her words intermingled with my own. I have left her words untouched so you can truly get a sense of the breadth of Kayla's soul and depth of her faith through the purest version of her writings. I pray that her words and this story bring light to any trial you may face. For we truly are sojourners in this earthly life.

-- Sonya Bonar

Contents

CHAPTER 1

This is My Story
(blog by Kayla, September 2013)

*"I've written a lot. I adore writing. I've written about practically anything and everything. However, I dislike talking about myself. It is the one topic I avoid at all costs. Don't get me wrong, I've filled journal on top of journal with life. But wait, sharing this knowledge? That's a totally different story. God has been convicting me of something (as He always is); God turns our messy lives into messages. I can **make Him famous** by sharing my story. We all have stories. They started the day we took our very first breath. Our lives are a book written by God. Each day is a page. Every decade a chapter. We were created to be read. We were written to put God on the Bestseller list!*

'God formed man out of dirt from the ground and blew into his nostrils the breath of life. The man came alive—a living soul!' Genesis 2:7

If that's not crazy, astonishing, and thrilling, I don't know what is.

Apparently, I am really good at putting on a poker face. I don't try to look like I have it all together. In fact, sometimes I feel like screaming, 'I'm not strong, but He is! Every waking minute Jesus is holding me!' It is because of his strength that I am capable of being strong in my weaknesses.

'But we have this treasure in jars of clay to show that this all-surpassing power is from God and not from us. We are hard pressed on every side, but not crushed; perplexed, but not in despair; persecuted, but not abandoned; struck down, but not destroyed. We always carry around in our body the death of Jesus, so that the LIFE of Jesus may also be revealed in our body.' 2 Corinthians 4:7-10

Before I begin my story, I want to exhort you to share yours. Your story may not sound exciting to you, but you never know whose life you can touch without sharing it! If it means anything, your story matters to me. If God created us to be full of purpose, shouldn't we have faith that He is using it for something epic?

I'm going to share with you mine. I would start with day one, but I'm 6,791 days old.

Eleven years ago, at the age of seven, I had my first epileptic seizure. I conked out on the floor of the Olive Garden Restaurant. Here's the catch: I was perfectly healthy, and nobody knew it was a seizure. We didn't even call an ambulance. I took a sip of water and finished eating dinner with my family. I felt fine after gracefully smashing my head on their brick floor. (OK, I make that sound much more exciting than it actually was.) Nothing showed up on my post-fall MRI. Not even a minor concussion. Clearly, angels do exist!

My mom scheduled an emergency appointment of course. She figured the whole thing was just a fluke, but it wasn't. You may be thinking, "wow, that is unfortunate." Well, you're wrong. That day changed my life forever. OK, now you're thinking, "well, duh." It was a good life changing experience. I'm still not sure exactly how it has changed my life for the better, but everything takes some time figuring out. Can I get an amen?

In the beginning I saw three different doctors. These three doctors proposed three different diagnoses: vasodepressor syncope, colloid on the 3rd ventricle of the heart, and a small chance the episode was a seizure.

I went through so many tests: crazy-EEGs, MRI, blood tests, the tilt-table test, the whole bit. I even wore a heart monitor for about one week. God was there. Holding my hand. He was upside down with me when I was strapped to the table.

My mom finally pulled out her handy dandy Taber's Medical Dictionary from the bookshelf, performed her own research, and basically said, "Let's take the focus off of the heart and look at what is going on in her brain."

Since my diagnosis of "absence seizures" has been confirmed, life has been a whirlwind. I've been tossed hither and thither. Since that time I've tried two alternative treatments to medication; The Modified Atkins Diet (MAD) and a Vagus Nerve Stimulator (VNS). Concerning the MAD, let me just say this. After six months of eating 10-15 grams of carbohydrates per day, I obtained a whole new appreciation for bread and an extreme dislike for cream and peanuts, which I practically thrived off of.

The VNS brings me to where I am today! Contrary to popular belief, the VNS is NOT brain surgery. Think of it more as a pacemaker for the brain. Well, I remember the day of my implant. I was supposed to have a history exam that day and all I could remember was that date, April 9th, 2009. Fast forward to today, 9/13/2013. Today I am recovering from the surgery I underwent yesterday to have the device removed. Why, you ask? I was given two choices: replace the battery, or remove the device. As of today I am fifty-one days seizure free! It's these little victories we must embrace.

A few days ago I received my OUTPATIENT NOTE in the mail. One sentence written by my physician stuck out to me: 'She has been approximately 40 days seizure free. It is not clear to us the reason for the increased efficacy." To doctors, these instances are just medical mysteries. I read this and thought to myself, "Clearly Jesus is at work in my life right now." I realize that while He is always at work in my life, I tend to only recognize this truth when I am having either a really bad day or an extraordinarily good day. Something about that needs to change. Whether or not I'm having a particular high or low day, I need to start off each day by saying these words:

This is the day which the Lord has made; Let us rejoice and be glad in it. (Psalm 118:24 NASB)

*God is consistent. That being said, I shouldn't "shelve" God. I **ALWAYS** need Him. I should never take Him down when I think I need Him and marginalize Him when I am under the impression that I can do things myself.*

So how is your storybook going to look? On the cover of my current journal, I wrote, "The story of how Jesus wrecked my life and put me back together again." He knows exactly what is wrong in our lives and puts us back together the way He sees fit! So why do we worry? We're still human. God recognizes that. We are extremely blessed because He looks at us the way He looks at His Son. Incredible!

Your story matters. How will you use it to change the world? Kayla"

CHAPTER 2

This is My Story

Choosing to start my story with the diagnosis of Kayla's epilepsy wasn't a hard decision. Up until that point in life, I had it pretty smooth sailing. Oh, I thought I had trials and tribulations, and I did. But nothing could compare with the next 15 years after her diagnosis at the age of seven.

I married my college sweetheart, Brian, in 1992. We both graduated from Virginia Tech. Brian was fortunate to find an architecture intern job in Irving, TX. We had Kayla in 1995 and then Isaac in 1997. After living in Irving for five years, we moved to Washington, which is Brian's stomping grounds. He found a job with MG2 Architects, where he still works today. In July of 1999, we were blessed with twins, Mason and Mackenzie. Wowzers! Talk about being busy! After one year, we decided we were done having babies, so 'snip' for Brian and that was it! Well,....as the Lord so often does (His ways are not our ways, Isaiah 55:8), He changed our hearts. Brian had a reversal, and we were blessed with Luke in 2007, Riley in 2009, Asher in 2011, and Elias in 2013. Count'em...eight! I have homeschooled the children off and on for 20 years. Each year has called for different situations. Our oldest are all on their own now, working or going to school, or married! We still have a full life with four boys under our roof. It's a blessing, but I can't say it's easy. In my "spare time," I love to study God's Word and to run. Also, I'm an avid baseball mom! I'm sure more of my story will come out in future chapters, but that's an introduction.

That day at Olive Garden sent us on a four-month quest for a diagnosis. Contrary to Kayla's memory, I did not schedule an emergency appointment right after the first episode. She had a couple more episodes after that, and each one was different. Once she fell straight back and basically bounced off the floor. Other times it would be a strange facial stare and she wouldn't comprehend what I had just said. I remember a woman at Olive Garden coming up to me and saying, "I think your daughter just had a seizure. We have a family member with seizures that resemble what just happened." That thought was in the back of my mind, but when I was then told over and over again that what we were describing "didn't sound like seizures", or that it's "highly unlikely," I started doubting.

Shortly after the Olive Garden incident, it happened again. She had an episode that was a fall, that scared me enough that I was worried about a concussion. I remember getting into the minivan with all of the children. I had called Brian to meet me at Children's ER. I was in such a state that when I got into the van I realized that I didn't have my shoes on. Thank God I thought to buckle the children into their car seats, as I don't remember doing that either. I was speeding down our road, headed for I-5. Sure enough, consistent with my driving record, I was pulled over by a police officer. He came to the door, and I was sobbing already. I told him my story, and by the grace of God, he let me go, asking me to "please be safe."

The trip to the ER was a total nightmare. We had to wait such a long time to be admitted. I have no recollection of what we did with the other three children during this visit! So thank you to whomever met us at the ER and entertained them! My whole intention of going was for someone to see her in the moment of her "incident" so my suspicions could be edified, but by the time we were sent to a room, Kayla was "back to normal." Nevertheless, I was *insistent* on them calling neurology. After pleading with the nursing staff, they finally complied. We had to wait for the on-call neurologist for what seemed like an eternity. Once he finally arrived and performed an initial exam, he was quite sure that what was happening were not seizures. He would not agree to an EEG despite my pleas. It was a frustrating experience not being heard. I just remember crying on the way home.

Ironically, about 10 years into our journey with Seattle Children's Neurology Department, that same doctor became Kayla's primary neurologist. Apparently, he only sees the most difficult patients. His specialty is working with children who cannot gain seizure control over the long term. I had a really hard time when he walked into the room for our first appointment, knowing that he was the first to discount my suspicion of seizures years earlier. God's mercy was definitely present, and I felt a sense of peace. Although he never prescribed anything that was any different than the previous neurologists, he *did* persevere with her care. After she passed, we received a personal card from him. I just pray that somehow her life and death positively affected him.

After the ER episode, we went back to see our primary care pediatrician. Fully aware of the ER visit, he referred us to Seattle Children's Hospital's cardiology department because he was the next to tell us it "didn't sound like seizures." So, off we went to Children's. Imagine the enormous stress during this difficult time, trying to navigate Kayla's medical needs, manage my own emotions, while also trying to arrange for the care of my other three little ones at home.

I went along with the heart monitoring, the tilt-table tests, and the EKG. Finally, after all this turned out normal I came out and asked our primary pediatrician for an EEG referral. Sure enough, that test was all we needed to confirm there was seizure activity on her brain. Thus began the search for the perfect medicinal cocktail which proved to be difficult.

A few years into her treatment, she continued to have breakthrough seizures. Breakthrough seizures are seizures that happen even though a person is on anti-seizure medicine. These seemed to come in clusters. She'd be very stable for weeks, and then have several spells in a matter of a few days. This led us to the Vagus Nerve Stimulator. For those of you who don't know what that is, Kayla described it as a "pacemaker for your brain." That is somewhat true. It doesn't give off electrical impulses until swiped with a magnet. The idea is that the person with seizures may feel a seizure coming on, also known as an aura, and swipe a magnet across the device that is implanted above the heart. The device has a wire that is wrapped around the Vagus Nerve. When the nerve is stimulated, these impulses are supposed to hinder the random electrical signals that trigger a seizure. Oh, this worked for a while. But it was always a challenge teaching the person/people Kayla would be with how to use the magnet, because, most often, she didn't know when a seizure was coming. Unfortunately, we didn't see a great reduction in the seizures, so we had it removed when it was time to replace the battery.

Next came the MAD diet. Boy, did that add a lot of work. The hope was that her body would go into a state of ketosis. The idea is that the ketones in the brain will ward off the random electrical impulses. Again, after a strong six-month effort doing that, no change. So, as she said, back to loving carbs!

The *'This is My Story'* blog post by Kayla is so dear and sweet. Little did she know that in a little over a year, her life would change again. And then four years after that, she'd no longer be here with us, laughing, writing, blogging, working, and trying to get through this life with what she often referred to as her "thorn."

In 2 Corinthians, The Apostle Paul refers to his thorn given by God. He pleaded with God for it to be taken from him. But God tells him, "My grace is sufficient for you, for my power is made perfect in weakness." 2 Corinthians 12:9. Paul then goes on to say that because of this he will BOAST all the more gladly in his weaknesses so that the power of Christ will rest on him.

In the margin of Kayla's Bible are her thoughts on this.

> *"Thorns are blessings. Like Paul, I have pleaded and cried out to God begging for me to be free from the pain. But recently, as I have matured in my walk, this thorn, my epilepsy, has caused my pride to be broken down. After coming to the end of myself and of options, I realized I cannot prove myself. I do not need to prove myself. Working and learning and doing are all good things. But Lord, you tell me to place my burdens at your feet and do all things for your glory. My thorn reminds me to declare your glory, (Psalm 19:1) and that my strength, physical and emotional, comes from you and you only."*

As I continue to heal, I have wanted to share the hope I have. Kayla is absent from her body, but present with Christ. I know I will see her again, whether in 40 years or 40 days. I will either be raptured or ruptured. May you find that hope in the words of this book.

19

CHAPTER 3

Transitions

In August of 2014, we had our Suburban packed and we excitedly embarked on our trip to Pullman, WA. Kayla, the oldest, was about to begin her first semester at Washington State University. She had taken a year off after high school to finish her degree at Edmonds Community College. With an associate's degree under her belt, we were confident she would succeed. Heck, she had made it through her college math classes with a "D" for done! Kayla was very thoughtful about change and wrote a post about it on her blog, "Coffee Shop Talk."

When Transition is Absolutely Necessary
(blog by Kayla, August 2014)

"I am back! These past couple of weeks have been rather busy wrapping up my summer classes and tearing apart my room. Since I'm currently in the middle of a transition, I've decided to share with you my thoughts, and why I personally believe transitions are important!

Before I go any further, you should know that I despise packing. I've always been one to over-pack. It's really silly because I could bring everything with me wherever I'm going and still be convinced that I don't quite have everything I need. For me, traveling is never enjoyable until the moment I actually arrive at my

21

destination. Nonetheless, transition and change are very healthy. Moving is hardly enjoyable, but it forces me to re-evaluate my life. Putting my life into boxes is a wonderful reminder of what I value. Trust me, I've spent the past two weeks attempting to determine what I consider the bare necessities—turns out those items are practically everything in my closet. Ha! While discussing this with a friend she commented "it takes a move." It really does. I'm not sure about you, but aside from a light spring cleaning, I don't annually do a deep cleanse of each square foot of my room. I'm just not a clean freak. I somehow managed to fit all of my belongings into the car. Well, my brother did most of the strategic packing, but I was an overseer of the whole operation. Trust me, had you been able to catch a glimpse of the trunk of our suburban, you would understand why this was such an incredible feat. I'm sure some of you resonate with my potential dilemma.

Change doesn't scare me. I'm simply not in the habit of taking new risks and attempting new things. I constantly tell myself that this should not be so. I suppose moving out of the house that I've lived in for 10 years is a perfect opportunity to break open that cozy cocoon of comfort. I may only be six hours away from home, but I may as well be in a different world in Pullman, Washington. Over the mountains and through the woods to Washington State University I go!

Transitioning is not easy because there is no telling what the future holds. But I promise you, change is absolutely necessary. Necessary for growth and perseverance and also for fun! There comes a time to start fresh and move upward and onwards. When you'll discover when that is, I don't know. You may not know either, at least not yet. Undoubtedly, it will be both easy and hard and with its own ups and downs. That is obvious.

You'll need coffee shops and sunsets and road trips.
Airplanes and passports and
New songs and old songs, but
People more than anything else.
You will need other people.
And you will need to be that
Other person to someone else,
A living, breathing, Screaming
invitation to believe better things.
-Jamie Tworkowski-

People are important. I deeply desire for everyone to find community. I've learned a lot about those deep bonds and the importance of both having friends and also being a friend.

Thank-you for continuing to read this blog and be a part of my story, despite my inconsistency and imperfections. If you write, surely you understand how impossible some writing days are. But whoever you are and whatever you do, I really cannot express how much your readership means to me. I'm excited to update you all on this exciting new adventure that is university! Knowing that you care about what I have to say is what keeps me going. If you're going through a transition, embrace the challenge, you'll grow and learn from these new experiences. Much love, Kayla"

Kayla was embarking on a brand new adventure. She wasn't just leaving her family behind, but leaving behind her years of ministry at our church. She enjoyed singing for the worship services in high school and junior high, helping at youth camps and bible school, or serving for her all-time favorite ministry, Isaiah 58. Many people would miss her willing spirit, but many more at WSU would gain from it. Here's a blog she wrote about her ministry with one of her favorite people, Kay, with Isaiah 58.

Did You Feed Me?
(blog by Kayla, September 2013)

"Meet Kay. Kay turned 86 in May. For over twenty years, Kay has been serving the homeless men and women of Downtown Seattle. Mission: serve the soul, not just the stomach.

Kay's ministry is titled 'The Lord's Table.' The location is at 6th and Columbia, directly underneath the freeway. On the second Thursday of every month, my church, Northshore Baptist Church in Kirkland serves with Kay. Our branch of the ministry is called Isaiah 58. Sixth and Columbia is home to many big hearts of the people who flock from the Union Gospel Mission, Pioneer Square, and all (literal) corners of Seattle for a warm meal of hearty Spanish rice.

In sixth grade, my friend and I were both looking for a ministry to become involved in. We stumbled upon Isaiah 58 after asking our youth pastors where we could serve locally. We've missed a few months here and there, but we both agree that it seems just yesterday, Kay was 80. I suppose it's because her stamina and passion hasn't wavered from year to year.

Kay thrives off of this verse: Mark 9:41 'Truly I tell you, anyone who gives you a cup of water in my name because you belong to the Messiah will certainly not lose their reward.'

A cup of coffee is capable of going a long way. Or tea. Or water. Or Kool Aid. Jesus constantly reminds us that the issue isn't a matter of liquids. It's a matter of the heart. The Lord of the universe can dwell in your heart if you allow Him to. He is the only free gift on earth that you don't need to work towards. There is no checklist to acceptance.

Seattle wants Jesus. They crave Him. They flock to 6th and Columbia because Jesus is evident in Kay. She treats them like her equal. She doesn't turn anyone away. She knows many patrons by name. More importantly, she bleeds the gospel.

Over the years I've encountered many fun characters. Seattle is a colorful place. I remember the man who could pop both eyes out of his sockets, the woman who asked me if I could give her pet mouse, Phoebe, a chocolate cookie. The regular who walked through our line and always asked for "Bill's Famous Tea." I remember gazing up through a space in the freeway where the two lanes came apart and feeling as if I were in the movie The Dark Knight. I remember when in junior high, Brianna and I collected donations from the youth group to buy Christmas gifts. I remember the British security guard with an Australian accent. Did I mention he dressed in a way that made him look as if he were the captain of a fine vessel? We've seen some interesting characters walk through those food lines.

*I tease Brianna endlessly for passing out too many desserts. To say Kay is frugal would be an understatement. "Just **ONE** cookie Brianna" and "Oh those will last until Monday," is common phraseology around her. Her influence (among others) has made me think twice about waste. I've poured perfectly filtered drinking water down the drain with my only pretense being that it had been sitting out too long. Thrown away food because I'm too full. Ditched socks because of one hole in one toe. Once monthly, for almost seven years I've served with Brianna. Last month I served with her **ONE. LAST. TIME.** (Indefinitely).*

New volunteers have made their appearances! Over the years as the youth have been a part of this great opportunity and we've begun spreading the word through social media, a large variety of people show up each month. It's always exciting to see volunteers come and go. But to see those who stay? Ahhhh, now that is quite a joy to see.

While Kay may never be replaced, the organization is looking for a new leader to take over all responsibility. The vocation has become an immense responsibility for just one person. We trust in God's provision. Always. This one's for you Kay! Kayla"

Kayla and her friend, Brianna, served faithfully with Isaiah 58 ministries for seven years. Once Brianna left for college, Kayla served one more year before heading to college. Unfortunately, a couple of years ago, the city of Seattle decided that no more ministry could be done at the location. What a tragic loss for those in need.

That drop off weekend at WSU in the fall of 2014 was full of fun. We had taken our sons, Luke and Riley, with us and left the two youngest at home. They were so proud of their big sister and helped haul all of the boxes and bins into her new dorm room. Part of the benefit of working so hard was that we took the kids out for a gigantic calzone at Sella's in Pullman. They are known for their pizza too! Ironically, one of Kayla's old soccer buddies was working there. She was talking to Kayla, and I looked over. Kayla had one of her blank stares, also known as an absence seizure. My stomach knotted up knowing that we would be leaving the next day. I know she was tired and probably didn't sleep much the night before we left. She was in God's hands.

The following weeks were spent with our family adjusting to Kayla being at college. I would check in frequently to make sure she was taking her medicine. She was enjoying college life and keeping busy. One unfortunate development was trouble with her roommate. Her roommate would stay in bed all day watching Netflix and basically wouldn't interact with Kayla at all. Kayla had shared with her before school started about her medical condition, and everything seemed cool. A few weeks into the semester, Kayla had a seizure while her roommate was there. This proved too stressful for the roommate, so she asked Kayla to move out. After a lot of discussion, we opted to have her move to a different dorm. Her room was a single, with the intention of finding another roommate. We didn't like the idea of her being alone, but we knew she had friends watching out for her. She actually thrived being alone. She could study when she needed to and sleep when she needed to, without a TV blaring 24/7.

I also know that Christ was doing a mighty work in her since she arrived at WSU. Kayla sought out a church community right away and had met some very wonderful Christ followers. In some notes from her memoir drafts, I found this when she was talking about her beginning time at WSU. To this day, I am amazed at the spirituality she possessed and her close relationship to God.

> *"Lord Jesus, I cannot even begin to explain or understand the great work you are doing in my life right now. But this is just how you work. You are unable to be explained. Forgive me for the times I have doubted your will. Thank you for the people you are bringing into my life this semester. Never have I felt so loved by any person aside from my parents. You have answered my prayers and sent people I can call friends, encouragers, protectors, and simply ones I know that care for me. I could be any place in the world and my health could be failing miserably, but I am so glad that you brought me here. So many prayers I didn't know need to be answered have been, in only a few short weeks. Help me now to use my mess as a message and my test as a testimony. I want to live never the same. I want to always show thanks for the great work you have done in my life. Taking the narrow path will never be easy. I can pray that I never stop believing that it is worth it. You have shown your faithfulness in so many ways. You have grown me. I praise you for who you are and you would allow me the pleasure of growing more like you. May I never grow tired of the gospel. The moment it does, wreck my life. If that is what it takes to keep me dependent on you, bring me to that place of suffering."*

When I start to ask the Lord, "Why do we face the trials? Why do we have to go through suffering?" I'm always brought back to the fact that we are not in control. God knows what will happen before we do, and the above prayer affirms to me that He was preparing Kayla for the days and years to come.

Kayla had also begun working for the WSU newspaper, 'The Daily Evergreen.' She would send me hard copies in the mail when she published. Her editor, Lance, would become one of her good friends and someone whom we still stay in touch with to this day. He was always very helpful to Kayla in the years to come, and I would often call on him when I couldn't get a hold of her. When Kayla graduated from WSU in December of 2017, he took some photographs of our family. A few days after she passed in 2018, he posted this on FB.

> *"Some of the greatest treasures of having become a photographer are the opportunities to permanently capture the essence of friends and family—the opportunities to make them feel special and to give them memories they're proud of.*
>
> *My work is my identity. But My work is also grounded in relationships. This dynamic creates a crazy beautiful life that has a lot of joy and a lot of pain.*
>
> *My awe-inspiring and close friend Kayla passed last week. These photos are from the last session we had together.*
>
> *While I've had a hard time finding a way to articulate my hurt, I've had hundreds of photos to smile and cry over.*
>
> *Kayla's friendship managed to pour over into all walks of my life.*
>
> *We worked in the same newsroom for years. I helped teach her journalism principles shortly before she quickly surpassed me in both dedication and talent. A kind force to be admired and respected.*
>
> *We attended the same classes for years. We encouraged and coached each other through some of the most stressful days of our student careers. Coffee and Bible got us through a lot.*

We worshiped at the same church for years. Our community fueled us and we fueled each other in the ways we loved people as Jesus loves us. Making friends that become family.

We gave each other family advice for years. As the oldest siblings of big families, we struggled together to learn how to love our families best. Fighting together to set examples that impact each member of our families.

We supported each other for years. Through social media, no matter how much either of us changed in character or aspirations, Kayla was my most ambitious and active encourager. Even my obsessions with pumpkin spice and Christmas.

What a way to live your life. What a legacy to have with people.

I love Kayla. I love her family, too. An immeasurable amount of people feel the same way I do.

Be thinking and praying for the Bonar family and everyone who adores them this weekend as we celebrate Kayla's life.

Matthew 5:4

Lance"

She was very busy and thriving during her first Semester at WSU that Fall of 2014. Kayla seemed to learn so much in those first three months of college life. Little did any of us know that this would soon come crashing down.

CHAPTER 4

Hope Is Hard

On Wednesday, November 5, 2014, Kayla and I were texting back and forth about the Apple Cup, and Mackenzie visiting WSU for that after Thanksgiving. For those of you non-Washingtonians, the Apple Cup is a bowl game between Washington State University (WSU) and The University of Washington (UW). Kayla was in good spirits that day and had apparently had a conversation with her friend, Arsenia, about her feeling of joy for the first time in a while. That night, she had Village with her church. Village is a place for students to get together each Wednesday and read scripture, pray, etc. I know Kayla was there because I confirmed that with Arsenia.

On Thursday, I texted, "Can you talk," and "love you," and she didn't respond. I knew she had a busy schedule. I'm not sure why the Holy Spirit didn't elevate my concern that evening. It has taken me a while to work through that guilt. But I have to trust God's timing.

On Friday, November 7, we went about our day as usual. It was a school day, so we finished up for the week with our studies, and the little boys played. Brian had been gone the whole day taking our boat to the place where we keep it for the winter. Finally, after getting the little boys to bed, we sat down to visit. Brian asked me if I had checked in with Kayla lately. I said, "Not since Wednesday." I decided to start calling and texting to check in. No response. Mackenzie had come into the room, and after hearing our concerns, she said, "Oh, her phone is probably dead. She told me she had to order a new charger." That comment didn't ease my intuition that something was very wrong. After no responses via texts and calls, I went on Facebook and started messaging everyone she was tagged with. No one had talked to her since Wednesday night. We finally sent a close friend a Facebook message and he went directly to her dorm and knocked. She didn't answer. He asked me if we should escalate. We then called the Pullman Police. This was around 10:30. It didn't take them long to get to the campus. After breaking the chain on the door to her room, they found her seizing. I then let a friend of Kayla's know. She was on her way to Pullman Regional Hospital within minutes. A group of her Resonate Church friends began to pray, and many went to the hospital to join her there.

Brian and I packed a bag quickly and were on the road at 12:30 a.m. I remember sitting on our bed trying to even focus on what I should pack. I couldn't think. I was crying and shaking. Our daughter, Mackenzie, was home that night, so she stayed with her little brothers. Arsenia was texting me and a nurse from Pullman Regional would call with information as needed. We arrived in Pullman around 5 a.m. We entered the ER, and went to her room. The doctor informed us she was "stable," but in reality, she was not. Brian and I knew when she opened her eyes that she was not "stable." She either had brain injury or was still seizing. The blank stare and bulging eyes were an indication to us that she was anything but stable. Plans began to transfer her to Seattle because Pullman Regional had no capacity to do an EEG or an MRI. And, as usual, it seemed like the process was taking forever. They had to call Seattle Children's Hospital and make sure her neurologist knew she was coming. I'm not sure why everything took so long. I remember thinking "for every minute we are here, more damage is happening in her brain." Finally, at 1:30 p.m. on Saturday, she and I were loaded into the transport ambulance and taken to Pullman airport.

I was feeling a lot of anxiety about how long the process to transfer took. We flew in a "fixed wing" plane to Seattle, Boeing Field. The flight was uneventful. It's basically an ICU thousands of feet in the air. Then another ambulance drove us to Seattle Children's Hospital. We were told to go straight to the ER, where they were waiting for her. She had spells in the ER where she would open her eyes and look around, but then go back to the blank stare.

Brian had to drive back from Pullman with no sleep. He arrived around dinner time. Meanwhile, Kayla was taken for a CAT scan to rule out blood clots. The CAT scan came back normal, which meant there were no blood clots. It also appeared that she had not fallen and suffered a concussion.

The other kids came to visit and had a lot of questions. "Will she be ok?" "Will she live?" "What now?" I couldn't answer any of those questions in the late hours of the night. But I did know one thing. Kayla would want us to hope. She had already written what we needed to hear.

Hope is Hard
(blog by Kayla, March 2014)

"Hope is hard. It's a fact of life. It means we're choosing to believe that there is indeed a light at the end of a very dark tunnel. That, my friend, is no easy feat.

Hope is counting on and clinging to what we cannot see. Hope is what we grab hold of as we're searching for peace in the middle of a war. Hope is not always comforting, but sometimes it's all that's left.

If Hope were a person, I wonder what he'd say or what he'd do. I'd like to believe that he'd take my hand and say "here's my hand, you can squeeze it." Hope would know that if I can't change my present circumstances, I'm better off knowing I don't need to endure the battle ahead alone.

Faith and hope work closely together. Without faith, how could we hope? How else could we confidently say, "everything will work out." Hope is the product of faith in something. In anything. In anyone.

CS Lewis once said that "Faith is the art of holding on to things in spite of your changing moods and circumstances." Sounds a lot like hope doesn't it?

Not everyone may believe in God or a supernatural being, but it'd take an incredible amount of convincing for someone to tell me they didn't have hope. We hope in our friends, our family, our circumstances. In tangible things.

However, I've found the most beautiful sort of hope is that which can't be seen or heard or touched, but still believed in. Hebrews 6:19 'We have this hope as an anchor for the soul, firm and secure.' Kayla"

While we were still in the ER, Brian and I knew that Kayla was still seizing. The EEG wasn't hooked up until around 9 p.m. after we had been there several hours. *Why did everything take so long?!* All I could think about was for every hour we had to wait on doctor's orders, her brain was getting more traumatized. Sure enough, the EEG showed there was still regular seizing. The doctors decided to medicate her strongly with anti-seizure meds, intubate her with a breathing tube, and put her into a medically induced coma. It seemed the only way to stop the seizing.

CHAPTER 5

A Long Road Ahead

Late Saturday night, she was transferred to the ICU. The neurology team came in Sunday morning, and they would watch the EEG until that afternoon and then gradually start weaning the midazolam, which is a strong anti-seizure medication.

(excerpt from blog by Kayla, December 2013)

> *"Embrace the unexpected journeys. Keep in mind the spectacular view from the mountaintop. Your journey is not the same as others. Cross out the words "always", "everybody", "perfect", and "failure" from your vocabulary lists. Remind yourself that if you continue to make attempts at living up to another's expectation for what should be God's plan for your life, you will never be happy. Worrying displays a lack of faith in God. He desires to do whatever it takes to "wake you up."*
> *"You are only human. Nobody is perfect the first time around. Or the second time. And even the third time. Rejoice in new mercies each morning."*

That morning in the ICU I rejoiced that Kayla was in a bed, asleep from medication, and that we had found her when we did. "The steadfast love of the LORD never ceases; his mercies never come to an end; they are new every morning; great is your faithfulness." Lamentations 3:22-23

We had a few visitors that day from our local church who came and brought coffee and snacks and prayed. One visitor stood out because she was a friend of Kayla's from WSU who also suffered from a chronic medical condition. She told us that Kayla had said something at church last Sunday that struck her. Kayla told her that day, four days before her worst seizure ever, "When you go through hard times and struggles, God is about to do something big." I immediately wrote that on her medical white board so I could expect something big. They started weaning the medication that afternoon. I begged God for her to wake up.

In my journal entry at 11 p.m. that evening, I wrote, "Dad is holding music up to your ear so you can hear Resonate playing their album. Mason, Mackenzie, and Isaac came at 8:00 p.m. and stayed until 9:15 p.m. Mackenzie painted your fingernails and never stopped touching you. We are all tired. Kayla, wake up soon!"

On Monday, November 10th, Kayla still hadn't shown any signs of waking up. Neurology came in and had a long conversation about their concern of global, or wide-spread brain injury. The MRI was a go, and by the end of the day we would know the results. After they took Kayla for the MRI, I opened my Bible and saw this highlighted verse. "You are the God who created the heavens and the earth. Nothing is too hard for you." Jeremiah 32:17

Kayla was brought back into the ICU around 4 p.m., and we were told that the team would be here as soon as they could to deliver their findings. As much as I claimed Hope, I was scared. God's presence was the only thing keeping me going. To pass the time while we waited, we braided Kayla's hair, had some food, and basically paced the floors. I tried to read my Bible, but the words weren't sticking. Pacing and praying was all I could do. Around 5 p.m. the team finally arrived with the news of the MRI. In a nutshell, there was not the global brain injury they feared. But there was temporal lobe injury on both sides. This was from the prolonged seizure activity. Temporal lobe damage can cause issues with memory and also with understanding and remembering verbal information.

She was expected to wake up, but there was no real way to determine the timeline and what we needed to do to get her fully recovered. In my journal I had written, "You're a fighter, you're hopeful, you trust, you're gonna get this. I love you and I'm praising our Lord for His provision for you and our family."

Later that evening more friends came to pray and visit. Mason, Isaac, and Mackenzie came. She opened her eyes for them! Good girl! That was the first we had seen her do that! Praise the Lord! The kids were tickling her feet and laughing, but there was an underlying current of concern in all of our hearts about what the future may look like for Kayla.

I slept better. I think my body was so worn out that I just had to sleep. On Tuesday morning, November 11, the team came in and tried to wake her. She had now been weaned off the strong anti-seizure, coma-inducing medicine for about 24 hours. They had no luck trying to rouse her. I grabbed her hand, squeezed it, and said, "This is mom. Wake up so the doctors can examine you!" She opened her eyes and smiled. I cried and thanked God for his mercy. That day they took out her breathing tube and she did fine. She was still opening her eyes, but not verbal yet. We had some really special visitors come that day, Jeff and Terry Clark. They were her leaders when Kayla went to Haiti in the summer of 2012 to help in an orphanage in Port au Prince, as well as other mission duties while there. The following is the letter Kayla sent out after she had gotten back from that trip to Haiti.

Summer of 2012—Beauty in the Broken
(letter written by Kayla, August 2012)

"I have returned from Haiti! Well, where do I begin? A thousand thoughts swirl through my brain when I hear the question, "So how was Haiti?" Let's see, how about life changing, eye-opening, humbling, exciting, joyful, saddening, overwhelming and inspiring. I want to thank you so much for your generous financial donations and your prayer support.

Monday, July 23, we launched our first day of vacation bible school. Nothing went according to our plans, but God's plans are always better, right? By God's good grace we were safely able to fetch over fifty children from a slum in Cite Soleil and arrived at Pastor Sylar's orphanage. All of these children are part of a school started by two of my team leaders one year ago, Jeff and Terry Clark. Pastor Sylar has 65 children himself in his tiny three-bedroom house. We were able to provide them with crafts, games and food and water. We broke down the communication barrier by showing our love through actions. It was a huge blessing. Please pray that they will continue to grow in their knowledge of Jesus and that they would remain healthy.

The entire trip I experienced a lot of what I like to call 'Beauty in the Broken' instances. This was certainly one of them. Many people see the broken in Haiti. Many people don't look for beauty. There is beauty in the broken Palace in Port-au-Prince. A stronger president has come to rise, one that the people respect and one that is doing his best to take action and make a change. There is beauty in seeing 56+ children leave a slum in Cite Soleil, the most dangerous city known to exist in the Western Hemisphere. There is beauty hearing and seeing the laughs and smiles of our translators and drivers as they wade and roll into the clear blue waters of the Caribbean. There is beauty in the 120+ malnourished children receiving a full plate of food and water. There is beauty in a man with no arms and legs painting a beautiful picture. There is beauty in a young man with only one arm playing some nice cool jazz. I think Christians and non-Christians alike need to jump at every opportunity we can to find Beauty in the Broken. Even in the rich country we live in, the brokenness is there, it just takes more looking to find it.

The rest of our trip was great and I was able to meet lots of really great people. I really want to share with you about my friend, Windy. It's hard to know where to start. His story is so inspiring. Windy is only twenty-seven years old, and when he was a teenager he brought his mother out of Cite Soleil. He had the world going for him. He worked as a translator for volunteer medical teams in Haiti, and last year he became an EMT for Port-au-Prince Medic One. That same month he became terribly ill and was admitted to Hospital Bernard Mevs where he was working. He became sicker and sicker. He has been to many hospitals since then and has had three major, but unofficial diagnoses: Tuberculosis, a bad parasite, and leukemia. But because of Haiti's poor health care, none of these diagnoses have been confirmed. And until he gets a proper diagnosis, he is confined to his country and cannot receive a medical visa. Six months ago he was not expected to make it. When we saw him, he was stable, but not well at all. He acted as a translator for nearly every single day we were there.

The day before we left we had the privilege of meeting with a worker from Medical Teams International to examine his health records. It was a somber day. His last diagnosis, which is looking pretty accurate, was leukemia. After the doctor sent him away and told him to never come back, the only thing he knew about his diagnosis was that it was bad and that he couldn't be helped. Nobody had ever told him that leukemia and cancer were the same thing. When he was informed of this he went into shock. He wandered out of the guest house we were staying in. For the first time he realized this could very easily be the end. He has been sick so long that his body would probably not be able to stand leukemia treatment—even if he could get it. Treatment is expensive in the states, but in Haiti it's thousands and thousands of dollars. He has not been able to obtain a medical visa and therefore, he is unable to come to the States for treatment. Right now he is living temporarily in his sister's house and caring for his mother. He receives less than one hundred dollars a month. But so far he has let nothing stop him. He is the one who had the dream to put the school in Cite Soleil. He is the reason why all those kids have a new goal and a focus. Now that he has been laid off from his job he is working on writing a book called, 'You Can,' something he started in a journal my leader gave him. On top of writing a book he is working towards his goal of learning 14 languages. (So far he knows French, Spanish, English, and is working on Portuguese.) He showed me what it really means to live like there is no tomorrow. He stressed that every minute, every second that he is alive, is a blessing from God and that you should live in that way as well. He truly believes in Exodus 14:14, his favorite bible verse. "The Lord will fight for you; you need only to be still."

And so concludes only a glimpse into my experience in Haiti!! Now the question is, what are you gonna do to help these people?! I'd love for you to prayerfully consider praying for all the children, for their health and safety, and that they would grow in the Lord. And especially for Windy, that we would be like him and take every opportunity that comes our way. Kayla"

In the above letter, Kayla mentions Windy. The following is a blog post written about a month after her hospitalization. Ironic that he met Jesus just six years before she did. What a blessing that they are both with Christ!

Two Years Later
(blog by Kayla, December 2014)

"In July of 2012, I travelled to Port-au-Prince, Haiti with a small team of high school and college students from Northshore Community Church. Our initial goal was to partner with a small orphanage located in one of the most poor and dangerous cities in the world. On that twelve-day trip, I met an amazing man named Windy Sauver. He had a passion for the children of Cite Soleil and a huge heart for Jesus.

Photo Credit: Luke White

He had an enormous impact on my outlook on life and my relationship with Jesus.

Windy was the most joyous person I'd ever met. His wide smile revealed pearly white teeth. When he thought no one was looking, I'd find him wearing his headphones and jamming to Imagine Me by Kirk Franklin.

At the time of our visit, Windy was also incredibly ill. Windy, unable to access reliable healthcare, was taken under the wing of Jeff and Terry Clark, our team leaders. The Clarks both work in the medical field in the United States. The Clarks, who worked alongside medical organizations in the states, finally concluded that Windy's illness was most likely leukemia.

On December 8th, 2012, Windy was finally able to see the face of his sweet Jesus. All of his earthly pain and suffering was finally removed and his body fully restored. My heart aches because I selfishly wish that he never had to stop listening to his gospel music and writing his book. However, I also am comforted because I know that he found solace and strength.

As someone also living with a disabling condition, I found his endurance, faith, and hope absolutely incredible. Ever since I had been diagnosed with epilepsy as a child, I consistently failed to believe that anything positive could come from my situation. His testimony gave me hope.

I relayed briefly these anxieties to Windy who bluntly stated that I was lacking the faith I claimed to hold. It took some time, but I eventually realized that he was not reprimanding me for any doubt. I think doubt is inevitable. In my life, doubt has always motivated me to seek truth and reassurance.

Windy told me that all the time God is good. I began to take his words to heart. Joy remains within reach and fear

> *should never dominate our lives, especially if we claim to be*
> *followers of Christ. Kayla"*

A little over a year after her trip to Haiti, (and roughly one year before the long hospitalization), Kayla wrote this about the Philippines. This small country is near and dear to us, as our daughter, Mackenzie, has been there on mission trips for three years with dear friends who serve there faithfully. Kayla had a heart for Jesus, which presented itself so clearly in her writing.

Constant in the Trials
(blog by Kayla, October 2013)

> *"I can't sleep tonight. My heart is aching. Breaking. Tonight*
> *my heart is with my brothers and sisters in the Philippines and*
> *those I know who have served there. Last night their world*
> *literally crumbled beneath their feet when a 7.2 earthquake*
> *hit Bohol and Cebu. When I hear of news like this, I feel help-*
> *less. Simply because I cannot be there in physical form. But*
> *God sent His son, SO THAT we can intervene. He wants us*
> *to come to Jesus with our prayers and concerns. For we cannot*
> *handle these trials on our own. My lack of faith is astounding.*
> *For God tells me if it were just as large as a mustard seed I*
> *could move mountains!*
>
> *God is changing me. Humbling me. Reminding me of how*
> *blessed I am to have a roof over my head and four walls enclos-*
> *ing me. Every day when I come home from being educated at*
> *school, I am welcomed with parents and brothers and a sister*
> *who love me. I have never known starvation or poverty. I've*

seen these things with my own eyes, but it is hard for someone so blessed with material items to follow the same narrow path. I have so much to lose by following Jesus. But if I really give Jesus my all, I make an eternal investment. I previously did not take this passage in the Bible very seriously. Then I started thinking. Just because I've given Him my life doesn't mean I've given Him my all.

I have a powerful God who loves and protects me. Always. Even when I stumble and sin against Him. I am reminded and grateful for all these things as all around the world many are struggling. Significantly.

But God is constant. He is the anchor to which I cling to and the one I must trust.

"For we have this hope as an anchor for the soul, firm and secure. It enters the inner sanctuary behind the curtain, where our forerunner, Jesus, has entered on our behalf." Hebrews 6:19-20

Lord, heal those who are broken, strengthen the weak, and call those of us who are able to you. Thank you for loving us always. Thank you for being the only One we can always count on; through every storm, up every mountain, and down every valley. Kayla"

After Jeff and Terry left on Tuesday, Kayla was moved out of the ICU and onto the medical floor. That was a little more peaceful with less beeping machines and scurrying about. There were quite a few visitors that evening as well. My friends made Kayla a wreath with many verses dangling from it. People could then write down verses or messages for her and for our family. It was a precious gesture and a treasure to read for the months to come. That night, she was still awake around 10:30. She still hadn't talked, however, she would follow people with her eyes and seem to understand the conversation. I decided that it was time for us to sleep, but I did ask her one question. I said, "Do you know who I am?" She shook her head, 'no.' That broke my heart, and it showed me she had a long way to progress.

CHAPTER 6

Who are You?

On Wednesday, November 12, I woke up early and Kayla was awake. I told her she needed to get some sleep. She looked at me and said, "I just keep waking up." That was the first time she had formed a sentence in almost a week! A friend whom we have known since we first moved to Washington came to visit that morning. This family has three children, all close in ages to our older children. We spent a few years homeschooling with them, and the kids spent a lot of time together. I asked Kayla if she knew who he was. She said his name. I was shocked! From what they told us about the MRI results, I knew that short term memory loss could be an issue. We hadn't seen this man in a couple of years at least. I looked at her and said, "That's right and I'm your mom!" She pulled her hand out of mine and said, "You're not my mom." Then we started talking about Isaac because his son and Isaac are friends. Kayla looked at me and said, "Wait, how do you know Isaac?" I said, "He's my son, and you're my daughter!" I happened to be wearing one of her bracelets that had been taken off of her in the ER. She saw it and said, "That's not funny." She said, "That's mine!" So I promptly took it off and put it back on her wrist. I then took out a couple of pictures that I had of the two of us together and said, "Who is that with you?" She said, "Not my mom!" I asked her what she remembered about her mom. She said, "She had the coolest hair." Haha! I stepped out and shared my concerns with the nurse. I asked her to go in and talk to Kayla about her feelings about me. I didn't want her to be scared. The nurse spent a few minutes alone in the room with her. She came back out and told me that Kayla wasn't scared of me, but she didn't recognize me. So I decided to back off on that conversation for now. It broke my heart, but I had to trust God. There was no other choice but hope.

This was my journal entry for that Wednesday:

"Kayla, since we arrived here on Saturday, I have experienced every emotion—fear, guilt, sadness, compassion, empathy, joy, pain, hope, faith and anger. But I have no doubt when you turn around, you will tell the world (as you told a friend of mine), 'I'm thankful for my seizures, they keep me humble.' God is a God of miracles. I have been so low this week, I have clung to his love and mercy like breath itself."

The next morning, the nurse began asking Kayla questions, such as her birthday and age, to which she was able to answer. When I was affirming her answers, she looked at me and said, "How do you know my birthday?" I said, "I know everything about you, I'm your mom!" She looked at me for a few seconds and said, "You're Sonya Bonar?" I said, "Yes!" Kayla nodded her head and said, "OK." I told her I was her number one fan. She responded with, "I've been blessed with a lot of second fans. I think we can both say that." Kayla has always inspired people by being a follower of Christ and giving Him glory for absolutely every good or bad thing.

About midmorning the Rehab team came in to evaluate Kayla for their program. They believed it would be a good transition before going home and being followed as an outpatient.

My journal entry that day:

"I can't believe we are already to this point. God has been so good. Kayla, I don't deserve a daughter as awesome as you. That is proof of God's mercy and grace and love that no human can give."

Brian and I spent time that day showing Kayla pictures of friends and family, and she recognized most people. All of the sudden she looked at me and said, "I haven't been in the Word like I should." That led me to read scripture to her. One big concern is that she isn't remembering short term events, like visitors from the day before. But again, God knew what he was doing and we clung to hope.

Rehab and Transition Home

By Friday the 14th, Kayla was transferred to rehab. The next few days consisted of about three rounds per day of physical, occupational, and speech therapies. It was very exhausting for her to learn to walk, talk, remember daily tasks, and work on eating appropriate foods so the feeding tube could come out.

On Saturday my parents arrived from Montana. That was a huge blessing to be able to let my mom stay a night or two so we could all sleep at home together.

It wasn't long until the questions started coming from Kayla about going back to school. My heart was breaking not knowing the answer for sure. At that point I told her maybe she could start journaling. I gave her the Watermark pen (a gift from her admiring Great-Aunt Lela) and a journal. She immediately began writing and I could see that again, her writing would be a big part of her healing.

The next few days were spent with more therapy. Also, a teacher from the hospital met with us about working on her first semester classes and trying to obtain some credits at some point. All of the therapists agreed that Kayla was making amazing progress, but she would need to continue some appointments as an outpatient for a few weeks. One of the ongoing concerns was still her short-term memory. Even when she would come back from speech or occupational therapies, she would have trouble recalling what she worked on.

She was still very focused on what to do about school, when to go back, etc. I was thankful for a pastor from our church and his wife who came to visit. At this time, they prayed for Kayla to trust the details to God, the therapists, and her parents.

The time to discharge from the Rehab unit to home came exactly two weeks from her arrival at the ER. Plans were made for our return several times a week for the next few weeks. A few days after being back home, Kayla blogged.

All Things Considered
(blog by Kayla, November 2014)

"Today I cried. It was the first time I had cried in a long time. At least from what I can remember and I haven't been remembering too well lately. Short-term memory loss tends to make life difficult in that way. Anyhow, I cried and it felt really, really great. I cried first with my sister and then with my mom.

Moseying around our room at home today, my sister asked me "are you OK?" I responded with "yeah, sorta, well actually no." Cue tears. And she said, 'that's OK. Nothing is wrong with not having it all together. No one is asking or expecting you to be totally with it.' I had a similar conversation with my mom. I am so thankful for these women in my life.

After coming home from spending two weeks in the hospital in Seattle, I wasn't sure the kinds of emotions I would experience, but after one week in I've mostly felt overwhelmed. After being home for one week, there is still so much to process. That is to be expected.

Two weeks ago, I had a seizure that caused me to become unconscious. After not being able to communicate with me, my parents started reaching out to my school friends via Facebook. Finally, after sending my friend Andrew directly to my dorm room, finding that I did not respond to his knocks, the police were called and the door to my room was broken down.

Before being flown to Seattle Children's Hospital from Washington State University, where I had been enjoying my first semester. I spent a short time in the ICU at Pullman Regional Hospital.

Things were bleak. I am no doctor, but I'm pretty confident that a lot of people were unsure of if or when I would wake up, and if so, what damage would follow?

Waking up, while clearly a great step towards recovery, was nonetheless very confusing. I didn't know where I was, who my parents were, or even what had happened.

In all of the confusion, there has also been a lot of clarity. I've had to rely and trust entirely on Jesus and my doctors. Jesus has shown me that my priorities are out of place and I also need to take it easier on myself. His presence has been so imminent. One of the workers in the hospital told me "I am so glad you have your faith!" I am too. I cannot even begin to imagine where I would be without my faith.

I have never felt so loved in my life. By God, friends, and complete strangers. I've also learned that just because God throws us curve balls in life, it does not mean at all that he does not care for us. This is not the case at all.

I feel strongest in my weakest moments. People have been calling me "miracle child" and more commonly, "fighter." And while I know this is meant to be flattering, I rarely ever consider myself either one. I call it being human. I am who I am because of hope.

When people ask me how I'm doing and how I'm handling everything, my typical response has been along the lines of "All things considered, I am doing great!" However, internally, I've also recognized it's perfectly healthy and normal to recognize that there have been large bumps in the road and recovery, especially emotional recovery, will only come with time.

Everyone, whether diagnosed with epilepsy or not, faces trials and tribulations of various sizes. Sure, the events which took place two weeks ago may not occur to everyone, but everyone has a story—one that is unique!

No matter what I write about, storytelling almost always becomes incorporated. I write and share with you only because I hope that it'll prompt you to do the same! So tell me, what's your story? Kayla"

As an outpatient, Kayla received a month of physical therapy, and several weeks of speech therapy. Along with this, she attended "school" as an outpatient. The teacher she had was phenomenal. He was able to help her organize her thoughts on paper so she could finish some assignments at home. Mostly what speech therapy worked on was her memory, her ability to plan, and working with her teachers at WSU on a plan for finishing some work. I was in contact with WSU's Student Access Center. Her liaison, Meredyth, was very diligent in making sure all of her teachers and professors were working with her to allow her to finish what she could. All in all, she ended up receiving nine credits that semester.

During this time of shuffling Kayla back and forth to appointments, I was so grateful to friends and family members who helped take care of the little boys. We were also still homeschooling at this point, so it certainly felt like balls were dropping all over the place. I had to let go of expectations of myself in order to help get Kayla back on her feet. By the end of December, therapists and the teachers were comfortable enough with her attempting to go back in January. We, however, were struggling with that concept.

Christmas 2014 felt extra special. We were so thankful that Kayla had made so much progress in about eight weeks. Being the driven one she was, Kayla began to talk of finding a roommate so she could return to school. She began posting in various chat groups on Facebook. By a miracle, we found Marcy, a believer in Jesus who had similar living habits as Kayla. Marcy lived in the dorm where Kayla started out initially. The thought of Kayla having a roommate who would be with her at least enough that no more than several hours would go by without a companion, made the thought a little less daunting.

Soon after the new year began, Kayla started packing her belongings. The idea was that she would work with Meredyth at the Student Access Center for accommodations, as in the past. She would continue to work on her fall classes that she hadn't completed, but at least be in proximity to her professors and friends. Brian and I were prayerfully considering this, but it was one of those decisions that didn't seem to have a right direction. We could send her back with a better check in plan and pray for the best, or she could sit in her room for a semester and become isolated and depressed. The lack of local friendships and social interactions had already begun to take a toll on her outlook, even in the short time she had been home.

CHAPTER 7

Crossroads and New Directions

It was early January 2015, the night before we were to travel over the mountain to Eastern Washington. We would be headed back to Pullman, WA and to Washington State University for spring semester. It was a place we hadn't been to since that long, middle of the night drive on November 7th, 2014. The car was packed, the little boys' care set up, groceries in the fridge for the bigger kids still at home, and Kayla was, to say the least, excited!

We were sitting in the kitchen the night before we were to depart. Kayla was sitting at the table, I was bustling around, and Brian was in the room. We were talking and all of the sudden I looked at Kayla and she had her head back and was having a seizure. It didn't last long, but it was enough to bring my stomach to a churn. What were we doing? Should we unpack the suburban and call this semester quits? Should we separate her from her friends and school? For the first time in a long time, she felt connected at WSU. She was independent and able to make choices about her whereabouts. When she was home, she was in her room until someone was available to take her somewhere, or on the rare occasion, someone called her up out of the blue to pick her up and hang out. Don't get me wrong, as a mom, I did my best to spend time with her and take her out. But, I also was a mom of four boys under the age of seven. She understood that and was grateful for the attention I could give.

Brian and I struggled that night. Taking her back felt unrealistic, but not taking her back felt sad. I knew that she needed her community to fully heal. In fact, I later learned that she had texted this to my Aunt Lela the day we left for Pullman.

> *"The community I have there is unlike any one that I've ever had in my life. So much spiritual healing has happened. I need that community there regardless of whether I am attending school or not. That spiritual healing has transcended over to my physical healing I think. Emotions, trauma, etc. It's funny how much I've learned in school that is not school related."*

We talked to the nurse on call at Seattle Children's Hospital Neurology that night. She said it wasn't uncommon for seizures to pop up after a prolonged event like she had. She felt that if Kayla and we had a plan for a seizure response (which we've always had), and her roommate was educated on it, then it was our decision. We went to bed, but honestly, I didn't sleep much. I fell asleep asking God to intervene. I was begging God to let her go back. Perhaps I missed the mark on praying specifically for HIS will.

The next morning, Kayla was up and ready to go. She left the decision up to us, but clearly, she had made up her mind. We decided to give it a go. The worst case scenario is that she would be sent back home if a seizure arose. In hindsight, maybe this wasn't the right decision. But what was at stake was her well-being. I think Brian and I were willing to take a non-life-threatening risk to give her this chance. Also in hindsight, if we would have kept her home, it would have been months of isolation, which would also have been detrimental for her.

We prayed, filled up our coffee mugs, kissed all the kids, and headed over the mountain. The drive didn't have the usual "back to school" excitement as it did in August of 2014. But Kayla was in the back texting her friends and keeping Marcy updated on our arrival.

When we got to Pullman, we went straight to campus so we could meet Marcy. The dorm is called Wilmer-Davis. It felt ironic that we were moving Kayla into the dorm where she started back in August. Marcy was waiting for us in the dorm room. She had Kayla's side all cleaned out and ready. We said our introductions and went to work unpacking. After we had most of the items in the room, we went out for pizza at Porchlight Pizza.

We had a long discussion with Marcy about Kayla and her condition. Marcy was genuinely happy to be a part of Kayla's success. We explained the medicine she takes if she has a seizure, told her where that would be, exchanged cell phone numbers and schedules. We wanted it to be as easy as possible for us to contact each other as needed.

We took the girls back to the dorm and let them settle in. Then Brian and I headed to the Marriott on campus. It was a fairly new hotel at that time and the nicest, closest place in town. We got a decent night's sleep. We had decided already to stay two nights. Making sure Kayla had what she needed before we left was important. We spent Sunday making trips to various stores to get personal items and things for the room. That day seemed to go really quickly, as I was anxious about leaving her.

Another important conversation we had was with her dorm hall Resident Advisor, Jenni. We needed to make sure that Kayla was seen daily. We also needed Jenni to know where the emergency anti-seizure medicine was kept. Technically, Marcy should get Jenni to administer it. Jenni was very kind and compassionate and assured us she would do her best to keep a special eye on Kayla.

Inevitably, Monday morning arrived. Brian and I got up leisurely because we knew Kayla needed sleep. We checked out of the hotel and picked up Kayla for breakfast. After breakfast, we had to say our "see you soons." I remember driving away and praying so hard that the Lord would protect her.

We arrived back at home at a fairly decent time. We carried on our evening and went to bed pretty exhausted. I checked in with Kayla and all was well. I promised to call in the morning.

This is my journal entry from Tuesday, January 13, 2015. "Well, we said goodbye to you on Monday. Tuesday morning I couldn't get a hold of you at 9 a.m. I waited 20-30 minutes thinking you might be in the shower. I called Jenni the RA to ask her to go check on you. Jenni said you were shaking and clenching teeth. I had her put an Ativan under your tongue at 9:50 a.m. By 10:30 you were still having a seizure so they called 911. Marcy rode with you to the hospital. Dad came home from work to drive to Pullman. But they said by 2 p.m. you would be on a flight to Seattle due to the time it took to stop the seizure. You arrived at Seattle Children's at 5 p.m.—straight to ICU. I stayed home and fed the troops, put Elias to bed and came. Kenzie, the sister of the year, put the rest of the boys to bed. You had been following commands, but you weren't when I got there. You are still having seizures where your eyes go back. We are still waiting for the EEG to begin."

That night the EEG was set up. By 1 a.m. her brain began to settle, only to have more seizures around 3 a.m.. This pattern went on for a day or so. Neurology didn't want to treat her as aggressively this time. So they adjusted her meds for a couple of days until she was stable.

On Wednesday, January 14, I journaled this. "I am just sitting here wondering why God is taking us down this path. There will be good out of it. Yes, Lord. All of my children are so important and loved. Why Kayla? Because you love her enough to speak through her."

By Friday, January 16, after a three night stay, we were discharged. Once we were home, Kayla was very quiet. She didn't want to read or write. I knew this was going to be a long road. But again, Kayla has always told everyone else in her life to have hope. It was her turn to show us. And our turn to walk alongside as the healing began.

CHAPTER 8

Healing on the Prairie

After being forced to come home mid-January of 2015, I could tell Kayla was just getting worn out. She wasn't attending school, didn't have a lot of friends around, and was becoming isolated. She and Mackenzie were great companions, but Mackenzie was in high school at this point and very busy with typical high school life. Kayla had her first semester schoolwork that she was trying to complete, and she did have a few people who had taken her out for coffee, etc. But the time she spent alone in her room was becoming worrisome.

The healing season in Montana began in the spring of 2015. My parents, Steve and Sherry Edwards, had been visiting from Montana in March. They took our then seven-year-old son, Luke, on a visit to their house. When they brought Luke back a week or so later, Kayla asked my dad if she could go home with them. "It's hard to have any peace and quiet around here." Agreed! Kayla was used to a lot of solitude being away, and coming home to a house of 10 proved to be hindering her healing even though she was basically done with her extended outpatient therapies. I prayed about it and came to the conclusion it would be a great opportunity for healing and to continue finding independence.

When Kayla first arrived, my parents set her up in an upstairs bedroom that looked out through a big cottonwood. She began getting back into the school work that she needed to complete. Once completed, she asked my dad if she could get a job, again, try-ing to find some independence. He approached a friend who was a principal at the elementary school, and asked if there was anything Kayla could do for work. The school was generous enough to set her up to help in special ed and also with math. I giggled when I heard the math part as I remember nights and nights of crying over Algebra. When she completed her final math class in college, she shouted, "D for done!" I'm pretty sure we both cried!

Things seemed to be working out for her, and I was excited she was in a small community where she could begin more emotional healing and make a difference. Here is a blog post she wrote during that time.

Montana Meanderings
(blog by Kayla, March 2015)

"I'm typing this blog post from a lovely little loft bedroom in my grandma and grandpa's house in Chinook, Montana. It's the type of room I'd imagine Charles Dickens, Herman Melville, or Ernest Hemingway wrote their novels from. However, I suspect my room is much more comfortable, cute and neatly organized than any habitat those drunkards wrote in.

I haven't visited Montana in close to six years. *Since then they've moved from the forests and mountains of Libby to the prairie land that is Chinook.*

The only sounds that I've heard this evening from my workspace have been nothing more than the sound of wheels and horns from nearby train tracks and a couple of dogs yipping and yapping at each other from across the neighborhood. But for the most part, my stay has been beautifully quiet and still. Simple.

Today I proofread a newspaper article. *I hadn't edited another person's work in months. It was a beautiful thing to return to my element. My grandpa didn't appreciate me marking up his completed article in red pen. Heck, at the last minute I almost packed my brand spanking new Associated Press Stylebook. But I didn't. Only because I had too many other notebooks, binders and reading material to strategically pack in my one suitcase.*

I've read more books *these past six months than I have in two or three years. In one train ride I finished 'Franny and Zooey' and over half of 'Catcher in the Rye,' each by J.D. Salinger. I'm certainly not short on reading material. Nonetheless, I cannot figure out what to read next.*

I shadowed my grandpa and followed him to his job at the 'Blaine County Journal ~News Opinion' weekly newspaper, the grocery store, bank, library, and credit union. Did I mention we were able to walk to all of these locations? And it nearly reached seventy degrees? It reminded me of Pullman, minus the hills.

After these important errands we searched around hunting for postcards. I'm a cheesy tourist and couldn't refrain.

I'm still writing, *in case you were wondering. I've been working on a lot of personal projects all of which include writing of some sort. I won't go into much detail, but this includes learning more about writing from a handful of my favorite authors and applying those lessons. For more hints you can see my Instagram profile. I have been doing my best to make the most of this short blip in time where I am taking a semester off from school.*

One project *that is not secret at all has been my Indiegogo fundraiser campaign I started for my service dog Charley —* *whose litter has not been chosen or likely born yet. Boy has that been an experience. Hardly halfway through my campaign and already over thirty percent of my funds have been raised. A couple of others include two different news outlets, two dreadful sociology papers and my church back in Pullman!*

Three. The number of times some dear soul has paid me to write. *Beginning and ending my job at the newspaper was awful. Not long after my first front page article was published in The Daily Evergreen I had to abruptly leave. I had to abandon many people and classes and activities I love. I know soon I'll be back. I'm not concerned about returning. I'm anxious about being uprooted again.*

Not knowing is an awful feeling. *Not knowing when or where my health could suddenly take a downward spiral. More than a feeling this has been a journey of trust. On more occasions than I can count I've asked God 'why me and why now?' I realize I placed so much faith and hope in moving out and being independent. November was terribly disappointing.*

All of that mess was redeemed. And through people and events that only God could orchestrate. You and I will consistently fall for the lie that good things cannot come through difficult circumstances. But God breaks our fall. He doesn't leave us abandoned. He intervenes. I say this now, after he's picked me up. I offered no pleasant words to God or anyone in the midst of my mess. It's OK to not be OK. Much love, Kayla"

When we were going through Kayla's things after she passed, I found a folder with some writings in it. These two "short stories," for lack of a better term, were both written while she was in Montana on pink sticky notes. I did my best to piece them together. These made me laugh, so I decided to include them as part of her Montana story.

The Damn Birds and the Damn Dogs
(written by Kayla, May 2015)

"I'm not sure what God was thinking when he created pigeons. Pigeons are damn wannabe doves. I've never heard such an obnoxious creature in my life. Had I known that a whole flock of them resided in the cottonwood tree right outside my bedroom window at my grandparents' house, I might have re-evaluated my living circumstances. Or at least location. When the wannabe doves finally pipe down—IF they do—every damn dog on the street starts barking. I've discovered our neighbor owns three small terrier mixes of some sort. They have fat Hitler mustaches and they don't bother waiting for the birds to pipe down to make their voices known."

Substitute Teaching at the High School
(written by Kayla, May 2015)

"I never expected to find myself in a position where I substituted for five math classes. I was terrified. I knew my students knew I had no idea what I was doing. I sifted through piles of homework sheets still waiting to be graded, trying to orient myself. Or at least find a way to look productive.

I'm a substitute teacher. I applied for this gig. I knew the possibility of teaching—even supervising—a math class could happen. Of course, I hoped, and even specified in my application that math is the last thing I prefer to teach. I thought admitting I had no idea what I was doing felt surprisingly refreshing. I didn't say it quite so bluntly, but they knew. Because I am still a

67

student, I know how it feels to be behind on work or utterly lost. I hadn't done anything, but unlike me, they weren't ashamed to work together, and dare I say it, ask for help.

I wish I had learned earlier that accepting help is a wonderful action step. There is the opposite, which is abusing 'help.' Also known as cheating, designating one student to work through all of the problems and whatnot. This appears a great opportunity until the teacher asks to see your work and explain how you've come to the conclusion, and you've merely copied the answer.

It is hard to cheat while writing. Probably impossible. There is no right answer to copy. The process is unavoidable. And if it could be avoided, anyone could do it. Very few choose to pursue the creative life. For understandable reasons too. The creative life, writing specifically, is very isolating. I'm not pretending to know more than I do about writing, but as a beginner, or shall I say, as someone who has only recently owned the title of 'writer,' I know as much. I'm sitting at my cluttered desk. After battling the blank page I decided to use pastel pink post it notes and write in short blurbs. Whatever ridiculous practice I must take up in order to find the right words, I will do. Kayla"

Time in Montana was good for Kayla, and for my parents. My mom walked the path to the school with her several times before her first day of work. It was evident to her (and us at home), that Kayla's brain was still struggling with short term memory recollection. My mom would stand out in their street and watch for her to make the turn a few blocks later. Then the school would be in her sight. She never would take a ride, even in the rain.

My parents would label the place setting for meals because Kayla couldn't remember where she sat at the previous one. She also couldn't remember where the cereal was just about every morning! Thankfully, as time went on, her brain compensated for the damaged temporal lobes.

After she settled in with her school job, Kayla decided to take on some writing opportunities with the local paper where my dad also wrote. The Blaine County Journal began publishing her work, making granddaughter and grandpa pretty proud. When they learned of the campaign we had started to earn money for Charley, The Journal decided to donate a percentage of the ads they sold for a month. What a blessing as they raised over $1,000!

Kayla ended up spending about half of the summer of 2015 with my parents. When she came back, I could tell it had been a healing experience, and that in a few short weeks she would be back to school in the Palouse with her little brother, Isaac!

Before leaving for school that fall, we held a small graduation party for our son, Isaac. He graduated from high school through Running Start, which is a dual enrollment program in Washington state. He had decided on WSU and it gave me some relief to know that he would be in the same town as Kayla. I tried not to burden him with that, but there would come plenty of times he would be called on to check on her.

CHAPTER 9

Charley

Photo Credit: Eric Foss

After Kayla was found seizing on that terrible night in November and then returning home from school again in January, we began to revisit the thought of her having a seizure response dog. We had talked about it in the past, but Kayla was not keen on the idea. So, we put that on the back burner. She had to be ALL IN or it wouldn't be beneficial. After she was discharged from the hospital, late in 2014, we had a discussion with her about getting a dog. She began to think and pray about it, and in late January, we began the process of finding a trainer who would specialize in a seizure response dog. Many people misunderstand this concept. A seizure response dog would not alert Kayla if she was about to have a seizure. But, the dog would be trained in how to respond if she did have a seizure—arousing, comforting, protecting, and alerting others. According to my research, there is not a real claim that dogs can be trained to alert a person of a seizure. However, over time with their "person," an animal may learn signs or behaviors that lead up to the seizure. At this point, the dog may itself alert the person of an oncoming event.

My amazing aunt, Lela, is a big advocate for Kayla. Kayla and Lela had a special bond. We were living in Texas at the time of Kayla's birth. We really didn't have any other family there in Texas, but my mom's sister and her husband lived fairly close. Lela and Dale would have us over for pizza, babysit on occasion, and spend holidays with us. She and my mom were the only family (besides Brian, haha) that were at the hospital when she was born. Lela coined the nickname "Kayla Koala" which we still lovingly use today. When Kayla went on her mission trips, Lela would provide a special journal or a practical gift. She likes to have "a mission." If someone has a need and she hears about it, boom. It's done. She was all on board to help with the search for a dog. Lela contacted trainers in Texas, Arizona, Idaho, California, and Washington. Some of the trainers required that the handler be trained with the dog. This wasn't an option because Kayla was planning to go back to school. So this narrowed the search down. We needed a trainer who would train a dog and then spend time with Kayla when the dog was ready to be handed over.

I will be forever grateful to Lela for the hours she spent on the phone interviewing prospective trainers. I knew I couldn't take on the task of finding a trainer. My youngest boy wasn't even two at the time, and well, there was so much to do as a mom of four little boys and three teens! I trusted Lela as she is very knowledgeable about dogs (at that time, they had three) and I knew she would be thorough.

Eventually, she narrowed it down to a training facility in San Diego, CA. The facility is called 'Specialty Dog Training.' Lela asked me to give them a call, so I did. The owner, Graham Bloem, is a qualified trainer. He admitted to having only trained a couple of seizure response dogs, but he was open to take us as clients. At that time, he only trained one service dog at a time. His other training included obedience training, behavioral cases, protection dogs, and puppy training. The nonprofit organization he co-founded is called 'Shelter to Soldier' (STS). He and the team at STS go to shelters and rescue dogs throughout Southern California and search for dogs that fit the health and behavior profile to become future service companions for post 9/11 combat veterans that have been recommended a service animal. I actually talked to one man on the phone and asked him a lot of questions. He couldn't say enough about his dog and the training. He said one day he had to leave his car for servicing. He decided to leave with his dog while the car was being fixed. He got a few blocks away and couldn't remember why he was out. He was having a lot of anxiety and starting to panic. The dog stopped and turned around. He took the veteran handler back to the car place where he remembered why he was there. He then called his wife to come and be with him.

We then confirmed that this was the training team we would trust to train a companion for Kayla. We were so excited when Graham contacted us with a breeder who had puppies due in May. Thus began the fundraising! The cost for a service dog is around $34,000. This sounds astronomical, but with puppy purchase, two years of training, food, intense one-on-one training for the last few months, and other expenses, it seemed doable. Kayla set up an Indiegogo fund (similar to GoFundMe). She posted her story, and we waited to see what would happen. Some friends from WSU and University of Idaho decided to make a video for the fundraising. Kayla and I took a trip to Pullman in February of 2015 to film. It was an awesome weekend with friends. We got the funds rolling, and started looking forward to May, when we would meet Charley. Why the name Charley, you ask? Kayla's blog post explains why.

Photo Credit: Eric Foss

Travels with Charley;
In Search of Funds for a Furry Friend
(blog by Kayla, February 2015)

"In my twenty years on this earth I've read hundreds of books. One of these titles was 'Travels With Charley: In Search of America,' a short memoir written by John Steinbeck. In high school, 'The Grapes of Wrath' turned me off. I never picked up another book written by this famous author after reading it in American Literature. If it hadn't been for the recommendation from the lovely man behind the counter at Re-Read Books in Edmonds, Washington, I wouldn't have looked for or found this hidden gem.

But man. I'm so glad this book made its way into my hands. It has reminded me to never stop dreaming, learning, traveling, and living. Even if I did suffer from a life-threatening seizure that nearly killed both me and my dreams. Life will have an abundance of trials. (I know what you're asking "why will no one stop telling me this?!") The answer my friend, is because very few people go through life without them. Don't view this negatively. Hard circumstances, hard people, hard questions have grown me and will undoubtedly grow you – if you allow them.

Steinbeck embarked on his journey across America so that he could adequately write American Lit. And besides, who doesn't love a good road trip? I've begun a quest of my own. The best part is that like Steinbeck, I'm meeting a lot of cool people along the way. Unlike Steinbeck, I'm starting out without a dog. Unfortunate for me, but I'm making friends along the way, and they all want the best for me. They've donated their time, skills, and finances. For that I am grateful.

Hop on the bandwagon with me! Kayla"

The litter of puppies was born on May 27, 2015. We were all so celebratory when we heard the news. We couldn't wait to see pictures, get details, and plan a trip to see Charley! The puppies were given different colored collars. When the training team went the first time to see them, they posted a close-up picture of each puppy. Kayla posted the pics on social media and friends began to try and guess which puppy would be Charley.

Well, purple seemed to be the color. After several trips to evaluate the puppies, Graham chose purple collar puppy, Kayla's Charley. 'Specialty Dog Training' had very specific personality traits they were looking for in order to choose a future service dog. I was thankful for the gift of discernment in finding just the right puppy for Kayla. In a few short weeks, Charley would be on her way to 'Specialty Dog Training' to begin puppy training.

Purple girl

In August of 2015 (four months after she was born), the girls and I decided to take a trip to visit Charley, and begin to let Kayla bond with her. We flew into San Diego and immediately found the nearest 'In-N-out Burger.' Kenzie and I had never had it. Yummy!

It was a short drive to the training facility from the airport. Charley was living with her trainer at the time. The trainer took Charley everywhere those first few months for standard puppy training. I remember asking, "So, how many hours a day does Charley participate in training?" The trainer responded, "She's ALWAYS training, every minute she is awake." I guess I hadn't thought of the day to day activities she was participating in as "training." The intense service dog training would come later after she had well established behavior in many different environments.

After our lunch, we headed to 'Specialty Dog Training.' When Kayla went to the door of the facility, a trainer came out holding Charley and said, "Meet your puppy!" Tears welled up in Kayla's eyes and one lone tear ran down her cheek as she held Charley for the first time. I was overcome with emotion knowing that in the near future, Kayla would have a faithful companion to help keep her safe.

After a short training session at the facility (they were working on basic commands) and some general rules, we were allowed to leave the facility campus with Charley. We took her to a nearby park and walked her around and played with her. Later we took her to the hotel. My Aunt Lela drove from Arizona to spend the weekend with us and also meet Charley. I was so grateful since she had

been an integral part in finding her. We had to sneak
Charley in the back door of
the hotel because we discovered it was a 'no pets allowed'
establishment.   Whoops!
Graham told us to give the
hotel his business card if there
were any issues and he would
explain what was going on.

Those nights we had her,
we spent lots of time going up
and down the stairs to sneak
her out to potty. She and Kayla seemed to be getting along well! I
remember Kayla taking a nap and Charley curling up next to her
like she already knew that Kayla was her person.

One night after we were done training, the girls and I drove out
to the San Diego beach. It was so beautiful at sunset. It was as if
God had given me that sunset to confirm our decision of pursuing
Charley.

We spent a lot of time just hanging out at the hotel and at the
facility since there wasn't a lot of training happening yet. Also
because Charley wasn't fully vaccinated at the time, we couldn't go
to many public places like the beach. We did practice basic puppy
commands and just made sure Kayla and Charley spent as much
time together as possible. We were able to take Charley with us to
a restaurant one evening. We sat outside and Charley curled up
under the table.

The time came when we needed to get back home. Kayla left a
couple of her clothing items with the team so that Charley could

have her smell linger after we were gone. It was hard to say goodbye, so instead we said our usual, "See you soon!"

In March of 2016 we got to visit Charley again at the facility. This time just Kayla and I flew out and my Aunt Lela met us there. We started out the trip by going to Kyrie's and Graham's house (the owners of the dog training facility). We had a nice brunch there before heading to our hotel to settle in. We spent the next few days doing a little more intense training. Charley had begun a little bit of her service dog training, basically getting exposed to all kinds of stimuli and environments. Graham said that the goal for a service dog is "a bomb could go off next to them, and they wouldn't lose focus of their person."

An interesting event happened on this trip. We had taken Charley with us to the hotel. Kayla was in the back seat, and Charley was next to her in a crate. We pulled into the parking lot, and I looked back and Kayla was having one of her absence seizures. She would just stare blankly and sometimes her head would go back. I knew what was happening so I got out of the car and let Charley out of her crate. She immediately moved right next to Kayla. It was interesting because Charley seemed to sense that something was awry because she had already begun pawing at the crate before I let her out. I was grateful that it happened because it gave Charley a sense of what her job would be. We got Kayla up to the room and she took a nap with Charley curled up next to her.

After that trip, we knew that the next time we would see Charley was when she was ready to come home and be Kayla's service dog. We were all excited with the progress she was making with training and with the bond they were creating.

CHAPTER 10

Back to WSU We Go

Before continuing our story about getting Kayla back to school, I'd like to share a blog post that she wrote a month before returning. I think it shows some perspective about how she was feeling.

OK?OK!
(blog by Kayla, July 2015)

"Yesterday, I finally told God everything that I felt weighing on my chest. The emotions I felt inside were nearly inflicting physical pain. I wrote it all down. While God knows all that is on my heart, I truly believe—yet sometimes forget—that He nonetheless desires us to come to Him with whatever sh** we're dealing with at the moment. To most people, being vulnerable is usually an admirable and brave action, but to humble myself to the God of my life is an incredible gift.

I've done a lot of reflecting on these past eight months. Reflecting, questioning, accusing, and comparing. After working hard in school for eight consecutive quarters before transferring to a state university, I was absolutely crushed. Devastated when my health spiraled sharply downwards in less than 48 hours.

I convinced myself-once I became cognizant enough to do so—that after all I had already been through, I wasn't deserving of a strong shove off the beaten path. A shove that screwed up my four year plan, and in my mind, wasted two years at community college for only three months at university.

By now, even writing this, I can trace a pattern. I dug myself into a grave that I almost didn't escape. Can't get a driver's license? Failing at relationships? Relying on nonexistent relationships to move from Point A to Point B? Let's direct all of that energy towards school. Now that I am able to control. I can either fail or flourish in this. All by myself. Shovel in hand I dug a grave six feet down and climbed in.

I should've learned, especially during the aftermath of these events, how destructive pride is. However, even now I find myself reaching for that shovel. Or, conversely, spilling out all my guts and expecting too many people to understand too many feels. Desperate for any word of encouragement or empathy. Those conversations—usually short—end with whomever is at the other end saying "you're such a fighter." Instead of swelling with pride and taking advantage of such a dramatic story, I remain deflated.

I thought I wanted something to brag about. But what I've always truly wanted is to be understood. For someone to reach out to me. More sacrificial relationships and less of me explaining myself and experiencing the need to say "I promise I'll pay for gas, I just want to talk to people again!"

After I was hospitalized and could not return to school immediately, I began to experience what I imagine many post-graduates go through. Community isn't only right across the hallway or the parking lot or next to me in a lecture hall. I must actively seek it. The get-well cards, flowers, balloons, and texts stopped coming. I realized how much I'd taken advantage of such a close-knit group of people that will always be different than those after college.

As I prepare to go back in less than a month, I'm afraid I'll have to start over again with new people. That sounds easier anyways. It'd be a fresh start in many ways. But relationships—strong ones—aren't easy. I'll admit there are so so many times where I am sure that I'm the one being more slighted than others. I need thicker skin than that.

Physical wounds are so much easier than emotional ones. Speaking of emotions, I received new pictures of Charley girl recently. School hasn't started yet but I'm already counting down the days until I am able to meet her. I could so use her by my side right now.

I am astounded by the generosity of you all. Every day, $34,000 becomes more and more easy to comprehend. More than the money donated, it's the sentiments shared by you all that gets me the most. I love that it has become an opportunity for people to encourage, empathize, and share stories. Kayla"

I have to say the time from November 2014 to August of 2015 almost felt as long as 2020! In all seriousness, a lot of healing happened and changes had been made. Kayla was packed for school, and Isaac was already there. He had gone early to join the Greek life.

This time, Luke and I helped load Kayla's belongings for the trek over the mountain and across the state to the metropolis of Pullman. I always enjoyed going there. It reminded me of the town of Blacksburg, VA, which is the home of the Virginia Tech Hokies. Both schools are basically what the town is made of and both are rather rural, with veterinary schools and a strong agricultural focus.

This fall, Kayla lived in a house with three other girls close to campus. It seemed like a great setup, as she could walk everywhere or take the bus if she needed to. We got her little room all set up on the second floor. I was hopeful that a room of her own with a roommate right next to her and two downstairs would be the environment that would keep her safe and surround her with friends.

Shortly into the semester it became apparent that this was not a good living situation for her. Some of the girls became more into partying than Kayla had expected. Kayla was firm in her faith and could not thrive in this environment. Not only was she not sleeping well, the house had no heat! That was not going to be tolerable in the winter! So, we set out on yet another adventure to find a roommate.

Being a part of the Resonate Church was the best decision Kayla made in college. Through their Facebook advertising page, Kayla was blessed to find a new roommate, Abbye. Abbye was actually a graduate of University of Idaho, which was just across the border from WSU. She was working as a nanny and living in Pullman. It wasn't long before Kayla was packed up and moved to an apartment with her new roommate and one that was a believer in Christ!

Kayla ended up living with Abbye the rest of that year and the next year and a half. She was thankful that she had found a Godly woman to live with and one who truly cared about her. When Charley entered the picture in 2017, there was no drama. Just love and acceptance. Abbye was always so kind to offer to take Kayla to the store or to church. I'm thankful that her last year and a half turned out much better.

For me, it was a fun season to have two kids at WSU. Mom's weekends, birthday weekends, girl weekends, and just anytime visits were something I looked forward to very much.

CHAPTER 11

Elevate

After a rather difficult re-entry into college life in the 2015-2016 year, Kayla had become extremely focused on another mission opportunity. As a parent, how can you tell your child not to go spread the gospel? Again we prayed and began to figure out whom to educate on what to do if Kayla were to have a seizure. She lived with several women who were more than willing to step in, give me a call, and help in whatever way they could so Kayla could have this experience. What is Elevate? Let's look at another blog Kayla posted. In a nutshell, the goal of Elevate is to spend the summer sharing the gospel. The students have a specific amount of time to find a job. There are certain stores and other businesses that have participated in the program. So the students interview and wait for the offer. Kayla finally got a job at Pottery Barn and a volunteer job with the food bank. The goal was to invite coworkers to beach parties and bonfires where they would hear the gospel. The following is a blog post written a few months after her experience.

Life Since Elevate: Part 1
(blog by Kayla, October 2016)

"Life since Elevate has gone by too fast. Summer is long over, but I am still mulling over everything I've learned. For those of you who don't know, Elevate is a 10 week-long discipleship

program through Resonate, my collegiate church home in Pullman, Washington. I spent my entire summer in La Jolla, California working a retail job at Pottery Barn kids at University Towne Center, volunteering at the San Diego Food Bank, but most of all, growing in community and in Jesus.

Explaining how Elevate continues to have an impact on me months later is difficult. In fact, I think my lack of explanation has been keeping me from writing. My last post that I wrote, I wrote in La Jolla. Elevate challenged me to my core, and as I expected coming back to school, the "daily grind" that Elevate pulled me away from has been far from easy. In California, I was blessed with having accountability and a Christian community on a 24/7 basis. Now that I'm back in Pullman, I'm struggling because experiences like the ones I had in California are rare and ideal.

I quickly placed a lot of weight and responsibility on the shoulders of my community to give me what they can't: the relationship that I want with my Heavenly Father. Elevate raised my standards of what Christian living looks like. I find myself now in a place where I realized that Christianity isn't about waiting for church on Sunday or Village on Wednesday, but having Jesus as a part of my life even when my Christian community isn't surrounding me physically. Experiencing Jesus in the quiet moments, after the pastor stops talking, the music winds down and my friends go on their way is something I didn't know would be so hard. I never thought solitude and silence would be a problem for a girl like me.

One of the lessons I learned after Elevate is that one summer isn't enough time to grow. I wish it were because growing pains are hard. This journey I'm on will last my entire lifetime. People constantly told me that Elevate was one of the best decisions they ever made. However, I always sensed that they wanted to add a "but.." to the end of their sentences. I understand why. For me, Elevate had a way of bringing to light everything I thought I had stowed away, hidden from the eyes of people that I know love me. Life before Elevate was easy because back then no one was holding me accountable to the skeletons in my closet. It changed everything for me. Everything was placed on the table, open for everyone to see. It was painful, how I imagine Eustace felt when Aslan graciously tore away his dragon scales until once again flesh was all that remained. There's a reason why this example from C.S. Lewis' Voyage of the Dawn Treader' is used so often. Baring ourselves to Christ and our community, any community really, is painful but His grace and mercy makes it so worth it.

'He has told you, O man, what is good: and what does the Lord require of you but to do justice, and to love kindness, and to walk humbly with your God?' Micah 6:8

Elevate was the start of a new journey for me, one that I didn't expect to begin and one that will probably never end. In the midst of constant community and accountability that I'd never experienced before, I learned and am still learning that no one else but me can take responsibility for my relationship with God.

My friend and room leader for the summer Meredith Brown speaks so much truth. About seven weeks into the summer she spoke truth that I am finally beginning to understand this semester. She told me that this year I'm going to learn what it means to be selfless and the person in the background serving. I wasn't sure what those sacrifices were going to be made but not long after I learned that I'd be in leadership in a freshman village (bible study) for the coming school year. I'm learning a lot. That these two years and counting of being involved with Resonate is not meant for me alone, but for all the people who still aren't connected to a wonderful community.

Additionally, I was "officially" placed on Gathering Team. Gathering Team is a vital group of people who help set up church in Todd Auditorium on Washington State University's campus and Schweitzer Engineering Lab in Pullman every Sunday. Not a whole lot has changed since last year except the title has kept me a lot more accountable and consistent. Another lesson I'm learning is that serving is rarely convenient, or it's not supposed to be. Service without sacrifice can be defined as good works or morals. Serving in these ways has been so humbling. I mean so humbling. I'm excited and also hesitant for this continuation of growth that is ahead of me. Kayla"

Kayla at La Jolla, CA

CHAPTER 12

Bringing Charley Home

At the beginning of 2017, which was almost two years after Charley's birth, we got news that the time was approaching to bring her home to Pullman. Graham worked with Kayla on some dates that would comply with her school schedule. At the end of March, Graham and his wife, Kyrie', would come to Pullman, WA with Charley. They would spend three days doing the handler training, and Kayla would then take a handler's test with Charley. At that point, Charley would be a certified service dog. We were all very excited as we had been waiting two years for this moment!

I decided to drive to Pullman and Brian stayed home with the other children. My Aunt Lela, who played such an integral part of finding Charley, planned her schedule so that she could be there as well. Graham and Kyrie' stayed on campus at the Marriott, which provided a great meeting spot and also the perfect place to do a lot of the training that would be needed.

The first day was basically a reuniting of Kayla and Charley. We didn't do a whole lot of "training" on this day, but we did spend some time on a few basic commands. We then took Charley to a local restaurant to have lunch. Charley and Kayla both needed rest in between training sessions. We decided that three sessions per day would be the goal. Any more than that and both person and dog would become overwhelmed. So we would do a morning, midday, and late afternoon session with plenty of rest in between.

One session we had to take Charley through several different stores to make sure she was not distracted. Because Kayla would eventually be taking Charley with her everywhere, many different environments needed to be explored as part of the training. Graham, Kayla, Charley and I set out to go to PetSmart. Charley walked up and down the aisles not even stopping to sniff the treats! Each time Kayla came to a stop, Charley would sit. She remembered her basic commands without much fault.

The big surprise came when we were in Walmart, which is right next to the Pullman PetSmart. Walking along, all of a sudden Charley squatted and pooped right in the aisle! Kayla was mortified, but Graham maintained a calm demeanor. It was actually quite a learning lesson. He said that this CANNOT happen during the handler's test. He pointed out to Kayla that before entering a store, she must always find a potty place. Charley had gone from the hotel until now with no potty breaks. So, lesson learned, and we finished the store tours for the day!

Another day was spent walking around on campus at WSU. Graham worked with Kayla on her use of basic commands, tone (must be somewhat firm), and remembering to praise, praise, praise for good work. I think that was hard for Kayla. She was forgetful already, so remembering to say "good girl" had to be practiced.

At the hotel where Graham was staying, we worked on elevator rides, Charley doing sit/stay in the hallway until called by Kayla, and going through different doorways. Charley was very attentive to Kayla, as if she already knew the importance of her companionship and the fact that this would be her lifelong responsibility.

The next big thing to train Charley on was the K-9 alert phone. Charley had been training with this in California, but hadn't done any training with Kayla. Basically, when Charley sensed something was wrong with Kayla, she would circle around her for a few seconds, try to arouse her, and if she couldn't, she would run and use her nose to press a button on a phone that sat on the ground. The phone would be programmed to call three different numbers and ultimately 911 if no one answered. So, we decided the phone would dial me, Aunt Lela, and Brian. We are all around our phones consistently.

Kayla practiced collapsing in different areas of her apartment. It was amazing how Charley would come, nudge her, circle around her, and then go to the phone. Of course, it was not connected when we were training. I felt a lot of peace knowing that we were on our way to a real safety plan for Kayla, and that we would never have to repeat the fall of 2014 again.

Kayla and Charley were now ready to take the handler's test. The test was basically a culmination of all the commands and activities over the prior three days. After the entire evaluation, Graham said to us, "I have not seen a more comfortable exchange." Kayla and Charley passed with flying colors! Graham then passed all the paperwork off to Kayla, said a tearful goodbye, headed to the airport, and Lela left shortly after. But I was having a difficult time thinking about leaving. I knew Kayla had her roommate, and now she had Charley, to keep her safe, which was comforting to me. Yet, whether it was leaving Kayla, or my son, Isaac, it was always so hard to say goodbye! As usual, we hugged tightly and said, "See you soon!"

Kayla finished out spring semester with Charley by her side. When summer came around, she really didn't want to move back home. She had some other church friends staying and she wanted to be close to them. So she found a job working for WSU Marketing. This job seemed to be a perfect fit for Kayla and Charley. A major portion of her time was spent walking around campus posting announcements for campus events; otherwise, she worked at her desk on different projects.

That summer was her first time to be a "partner" with Charley. As much of a blessing as it was to have Charley for companionship and safety, there were some challenges as well. Kayla was always so gracious, but was also beginning to learn that most people have no clue how to respond to someone with a service dog. The following is a blog she wrote about this particular subject. Learn and enjoy!

Life Since Charley
(blog by Kayla, May 2017)

"I've had Charley for almost two months now. For over two years I had waited for March 23rd, 2017. I had a gender reveal on Instagram. She's watching me write this blog post right now.

I knew it wasn't going to be all cuddles and kisses...but it wasn't until I got her that I realized just how uneducated people are...not only in regards to epilepsy, but to all invisible diseases and the responsibilities and tasks that vary between service dogs, emotional/therapy animals, and pets with vests.

I love Charley, but since she goes everywhere with me, I've answered some pretty ridiculous questions, and I'm not one to call most questions ridiculous. According to ADA laws, I'm only obligated to answer two questions, (1) is the dog a service animal required because of a disability, and (2) what work or task has the dog been trained to perform. Staff cannot ask about the person's disability, require medical documentation, require a special identification card or training documentation for the dog, or ask that the dog demonstrate its ability to perform the work or task.

Despite the intrusive nature of some questions I've received, I've yet to come up with a polite way to decline and continue on with a conversation. Here are some of the questions I've encountered:

- *"Where did you buy the jacket (vest) for your dog? I want to get one for my dogs." This one made me really sad. When people buy vests so they can take their pets with them into establishments, it's like a smack in the face. It delegitimizes the seriousness of someone's disease—whether that be physical, emotional, or both. A vest used to carry a certain weight. That weight has been replaced with distrust and has raised a plethora of questions, and no one is fact—checking answers:*
- *"Do you have to take her everywhere?"*
- *"Are you training her?"*
- *"What does she do?"*
- *"How old is she?"*
- *"What breed is she?"*
- *"Can I pet her?"*
- **Pity smile**
- **Pets Charley**

By acquiring a service animal, you commit to prioritizing your health despite insecurities about having a dog with you. A dog wearing a vest can send either one of two messages: 1) You have a disability (illness) 2) You are obsessed with your pet enough to pretend you have a legitimate need (to an extent that you feel comfortable with). When people are inconsistent with where they bring their dog, it gives the impression that it's an option. Only nineteen states punish individuals for fake service dogs .

A few weeks ago, I was in a school office building returning rental stuff that I needed for a class. Out of an office bolted a small, barking dog that was off-leash. I was supposed to take the handler's word for it when she said it was a Pet Partner, an organization I had to research later. In Pullman, leash laws are required for all dogs when away from the owner's private property. Service dogs get no special treatment in this area.

Since getting Charley, we have conquered some huge fears/ transitions together. She's adjusted to the classroom setting, my new workplace on campus, and my strange anxiety about taking her with me to the grocery store.

Life only screeches to a halt if we let change cripple us, which is easier than I'd like to admit. Don't let silly questions become personal insults. And don't let insecurities trap you in fear. Kayla"

Here is a "Leave a Reply" on her post:

January 5, 2018 at 1:28 p.m.
Kayla, thanks for sharing this. I know it's been a while since you've posted this but it was fascinating and incredibly insightful from your perspective and the perspective of those who have to have service dogs along with them. Also, I didn't think at all about folks using vests on their dogs to get a pass like that, dang that's disappointing. Anyways, thanks for sharing this. Learned a lot.

CHAPTER 13

A Season to Remember

December 2017 Kayla graduated with a Bachelor's in Communication and Media Production from WSU. This day had been long-awaited, and at times, I'll be honest, doubted. The obstacles Kayla (and the family) overcame to get here made it a fine celebration. Little brothers adorned in their Sunday best (which basically meant no sweats or gym shorts), proud older brothers and younger sister, grandparents, aunts, and cousins traveled from as far as Arizona to attend. December graduations are less crowded, but it was still quite a task to find a restaurant to seat 18 people! However, the day went on without a hitch except for one set of grandparents taking bedbugs home. But, overall, the day was a joyous and memorable occasion.

One of my favorite memories of the day is this photo taken by our good friend, Lance. He is a freelance photographer and entrepreneur and captured Kayla and her siblings beautifully! (He also gets the photo credit of Kayla and Charley on the dedication page.)

Photo credit: Lance Lijewski

Shortly after graduating from WSU, Kayla came home to Lynnwood to apply for jobs. This girl was a go-getter. Before Christmas, she secured a job in Ellensburg as "Breaking News" reporter for The Daily Record.

Just after the new year, we made the move to Ellensburg. Kayla was able to find roommates who were attending Central Washington University, and were also a part of the Resonate church plant that came from Pullman.

Working at The Daily Record proved itself challenging. Learning a new community along with a new job brought many joys and tears for Kayla. Disengaging from the stories was a challenge for her compassionate heart.

Two stories stand out in my memory that brought her to her knees, and also gave her opportunities to be a light for Christ and his healing.

One incident occurred in August of 2018. A 13-year-old boy was killed and four other kids were injured in a collision outside of Cle Elum (a few miles from Ellensburg). Kayla had the job of interviewing the officer that had been on the scene. The driver had been under the influence of prescription medication. None of his passengers (four boys ages 12 and 13) were wearing belts. Oddly enough, the driver managed to remember to wear his.

This affected her in that it brought doubt in how something so awful can be used for good. Ironically, this incident led me to correspond with the deceased boys' mother. She was a friend of an acquaintance and we were introduced via email. Through this, we were later able to encourage each other after both of us had experienced such great loss. In the deep grief it is a huge blessing to have someone with whom you can empathize – someone who truly knows the pain.

Another story that stands out is an unfortunate event involving two cadets that were part of the CWU (Central Washington University) ROTC program. About eight weeks before Kayla passed, she reported on this story. When the detectives arrived after a call, two males, 21 and 22 years of age, were found dead from gunshot wounds. It appeared that the 22-year-old died after being accidentally shot by the 21-year-old, and then the 21-year-old died of a self-inflicted gunshot wound.

This story hit hard for Kayla. But it also opened up opportunities for being a light in the darkness. One such story was told at her memorial service.

This was the story one of the cadets' female friends told at Kayla's memorial service:

"I need you to understand how much she meant to me. She is the only reason I am still here. One day I was walking across campus, she had just gotten off work or was going somewhere but she saw me and I was crying. She asked me how I was doing and I shrugged it off and said I was fine. She didn't accept that, she sat me down and asked me what was going on and I poured my heart out to her. I was ready to take my own life, she sat with me for hours and prayed for me and cried with me. If she hadn't stopped me that day I would not be here."

A couple of months later, I got a message from the same girl. It's just another affirmation to me that Kayla's life, although short, was lived with an eternal perspective. Her message to me said this:

"Good afternoon, just wanted to share this with you. I met a girl a few days ago who reminded me a lot of Kayla, personality-wise they were very similar and in a few other ways. I mentioned this to her, and she asked me who Kayla was and I started to tell her about Kayla, where I met her and who Kayla was as a person. This conversation ended with me and the girl I was talking to crying, I got to share the gospel with this girl, and she is coming to church with me tomorrow."

After a few months on the job, Kayla decided to make Ellensburg her home. She had been wavering on whether to stay at The Daily Record during the transition period of editors, and also feeling discouraged about the staff turnover. However, I know she had developed a heart for the community and the people of Ellensburg.

Soul Check: Being Still
(blog by Kayla, July 2018)

"These past few months have been a whirlwind.
You guys, this world just does not stop (I realize this is not new information).

You'd think as a human and especially as a reporter that would stop surprising me.

It still stops me in my tracks.

The truth is I love my job, but this week I realized I've neglected my soul in an effort to pursue my day job, which I'm thankful to love.

I go into situations with good intentions and come out on the other side beat up like a tumbleweed on the side of the road.

(Maybe it's this Ellensburg wind finally getting to my head, who knows).

In all seriousness, I'm a go-getter, but am very slow to establish boundaries in many areas of my life, which leads to a crash-and-burn situation.

I've been here before.

Burnout is when you think you're doing right by yourself by paying your dues in your workplace, school, whatever it may be for you in this season of life you're in but it happens to everyone. It's part of our world's culture, but it didn't have to be part of mine or yours. And praise God this is true.

I've learned some things since this last happened and one of them is taking care of your soul.

I moved so often in college that I just stopped trying to settle in.

Because you know, if you just stop trying, you'd think maybe the next time it wouldn't be so painful.

I didn't realize how wrong I was until my community surrounded me with love and helped me move, no questions asked. Fam, for our souls to heal and feel, they need to be accessible.

This was such a huge kairos moment for me.

What I realized in this moment and what maybe you'll

realize after reading this, is we too often discredit ourselves from the abundance of blessings God desires to bestow upon us because we tell ourselves we're too needy, not ready...the list goes on and on.

There are many characteristics about God, but I think my all-time favorite is that he doesn't have baggage.

Like his Son, Jesus, he is holy and blameless. I love my community, and as much as I love them and they love me, only God can place those holy desires in my heart. No number of people, amount of talking or listening can replace being near and still to and with Him.

Because community is such a good thing, it's easy for the devil to sneak in like the serpent he is and whisper that so long as we have people, maybe that can replace God.

Too often I've gone to my community first instead of my savior and praise God they've had the wisdom to remind me only God can change my heart. They haven't said "oh yeah, I've been a Christian longer."

The best community points you back to God. Again, and again and again.

The best community says no one ever said you had to go this alone. Or, these burdens, they're self-inflicted.

Christ is not of this world which is why he makes the ultimate savior. He's the only one who knows you and I better than ourselves.

'The Lord will fight for you, you need only to be still' (Exodus 14:14) You can be a fighter, and you should put in the work, but at the end of the day, we need to be still and remember the battle has already been won.

For the first time in a long time, I let myself put down roots. I said no to fear, bought some furniture, and signed a year-long lease in Ellensburg.

It takes more than that to make a space a home, but after time and a lot of work, God showed me look at all you have, right here in front of you.

Don't run away merely because you're afraid of losing it. I'm not talking about fear of physical objects. We all know a table is a table, etc. However, those things do help create a space to be still with God and see His faithfulness.

My sister reminded me that wherever Jesus was when He walked this earth He created a space to go and talk to his Father. The disciples thought He was crazy and were constantly impatient with Him, but He understood the value of that stillness no matter where He was, He made time.

He understood things would always be crazy and the time would never be just right, but it was vital to his soul and to his ministry.

Living with one foot in the world and one foot with Jesus will never work because he tells us part of our identity in Christ is we are a holy people, precious to God, and he has called us to be set apart. Kayla"

After starting her job at The Daily Record, Kayla spent less and less time blogging. Sadly, for me and the rest of her followers, this was her last "Coffee Shop Talk" blog post. Because I believe her writing is inspiring and encouraging, the blog is still active and anyone can go to www.kaylabonar.com to read her posts.

CHAPTER 14

Everything Changed

The Daily Record had been in somewhat of a disarray for a few months. Their previous editor left for another job, and there had been a few other writers that had moved on. For a while Kayla was covering beats that she wasn't familiar with. But as she always did, she persevered and made the best of the situation. Right before she passed, things were looking up at The Daily Record. This was the last FB post written by Kayla. The post was written on December 5, 2018, at 10:27 p.m.

> *"After several months of turnover and big transitions, the Daily Record newsroom is staffed once again with a full-time photographer, sports editor, court/city/local reporter and our Editor-in-Chief. In the past six months I had three or four high profile superior court cases without having ever stepped foot in a courtroom in a professional or private capacity. Week-long wild-land fires and structure fires at different points in the year. 10-15 hour days. (Fire season is all year folks). I'm saying this not to brag but because I was literally juggling so many different types of stories and was unsure if I was doing any of them well. Here's to a new year. We rallied. Also, I would just like to emphasize that folks who left moved on to bigger better things, and we did not make any cuts. We are a (newsroom) staff of six!"*

Unfortunately, after Kayla's passing in the night, the newsroom was back to a staff of five...

Divine Blessings

The last time I visited Ellensberg was November 7, 2018, nearly one month to the day that Kayla went to be with the Lord. I had been feeling this urgency to get the little boys over to see Kayla in her 'element.' So, we planned a day when we were free from any obligations and took a road trip! Ellensberg is roughly 100 miles from our house. We left early in the morning so we would have a good amount of time to relax and just some unhurried time together. Kayla said she could be off work by midmorning.

It was such a sweet trip. We picked her and Charley up from work, stopped to pick up Taco Bell, and went to her little house to visit. Asher asked her to warm up his taco in the microwave. She apparently didn't learn her microwave fundamentals because she left the taco in so long it was like rubber! We laughed about that together. The boys wanted to color, so we hunted around for anything other than a black pen! Instead we decided to play cards, but, of course, she didn't have a deck of cards! I suppose you forget what it's like to be young and independent with no need for things like crayons and cards. So, we went to the park instead and then we stopped to pick up a deck of cards on the way back to her house. I took the four boys to see her office, and they all took a turn sitting in her chair. We walked around some of the shops downtown. After a fun afternoon, we dropped her off at her house, and said our "see you soons."

The next time I was at her house was to clean out her belongings. Thanksgiving break of 2018 turned out to be a wonderful family week. Kayla got a ride home from Ellensburg, and Mackenzie picked her up at the designated meeting spot. We had some good visiting time. We had just moved into a new house, and she and Kenzie would share a room as they had growing up. This time, though, Kayla's mattress was on the floor! She didn't care. She and Kenzie spent hours there, talking, laughing, reading, and crocheting. In fact, their big "Black Friday" adventure was dedicated to buying lots of new yarn for future projects and Christmas gifts!

Thanksgiving Day was wonderful. I had noticed Kayla interacting with everyone present. The entire weekend I noticed her taking time to spend with each little brother. She was full of hugs and just seemed happy. When it was time for her to go, we said our "see you soons"—not knowing this would be our last time to hug her.

That Thursday morning, December 6th, 2018 was a pretty typical morning. I talked to Kayla the night before and she told me she was going to take Thursday off for a "mental day" as she put it. She said she hadn't been feeling so great. She wasn't necessarily sick, she apparently just needed to slow down and process some things. Her coworker, Robyn, had spent some time with her that Wednesday evening. Robyn had also graciously gone grocery shopping for her. Knowing all of this, I wasn't alarmed when I hadn't gotten a notification on my phone that she had taken her medicine that Thursday morning. I took Elias to school, Brian's dad had picked up Asher for a haircut, and the other boys were working on their schoolwork.

I had just started doing some dishes when I got a text from her coworker, Robyn. She was concerned because she hadn't heard from Kayla. I told her I was letting her sleep in a bit and would check in on her again soon.

Around 10:30 a.m. I started texting her. No response. I elevated to calling, but still, no phone picked up. I called Robyn and asked her to go check on her. Just the night before, when Robyn was with Kayla, she had given Robyn a key to her house. Kayla's little "house"—which was basically a garage-turned-apartment—had its own key. While she had some roommates in the big house, I had wanted someone else to have a key and had been asking Kayla to do that for months! I am convinced it was God who nudged Kayla to give Robyn that key.

A long while went by and I hadn't heard from Robyn. The pit of my stomach started churning and I was feeling weak. I called her and said, "Well, is she OK?" Robyn was silent. "Is she unconscious?" I asked. She responded with, "I think it might be worse than that." She said she had already called 911. I asked her to call me back when the emergency responders arrived. I sat on the couch and started shaking. I think at that point, I already knew in my heart what had happened. A few minutes later, Robyn called me back. She and the officer on the scene confirmed the worst possible news of my life. Our precious Kayla was gone.

(I wrote this on 12/7/2018) Kayla Nicole Bonar passed away in her sleep. I can't believe I am writing these words. This burden I have right now feels like a giant elephant on my shoulders. I'm the one who checked in on her twice a day from afar, took her calls when she needed a shoulder to cry on, had to be the discerning one. Should I have seen something different about the night of 12/5 when we talked on the phone? She told me she had an emotional day. She said she spent time with her staff. Processing all of the changes led her to a "healthy breakdown." Believing finally that she had graduated from college and had a real job. She is often in an upset state of mind when she calls me, so this was nothing out of the ordinary. I listened to her talk for quite some time, although I wonder how much my mind wandered. Why is it that we don't take advantage of talking with people until it's too late? She talked about work mostly, the new girl who started, etc. Robyn, the wonderful "mom of Ellensburg," who worked in advertising at the paper, had brought her home after the "hang out." Robyn then went to the store for her and bought her food because she wasn't feeling well. "Robyn is like you mom. She buys things I would never buy, but things I've wanted to try." Kayla was tired and had decided to take the next day off.

What was it that I missed during that phone call? Did the Holy Spirit try to nudge me? Should I have gotten in the car knowing she wasn't feeling one hundred percent? Back to the phone call. We said goodbye and "I love you." Around 10 p.m. that night I checked to make sure she had taken her medicine. She said she had a headache. Again this is not completely unusual. She had no missed medicine doses, nothing alerted me like something she said not making sense, or "off" speech. Maybe I'm trying to convince myself of what we already know. Our days are numbered. "Your eyes saw my unformed substance; in your book were written, every one of them, the days that were formed for me, when as yet there were none of them." Psalm 139:16. Kayla's death wasn't a shock to God. He knew the day before she was even formed in my womb.

Early Grief

The early days after her death are pretty much a blur. My brain was so overwhelmed. There's the pressure to start planning some kind of memorial, take care of her things, contact people, etc. The list felt so heavy. All I wanted to do was sit and wrap in a blanket with her blog, Bible, and journals. But life had to be lived. We had to grieve as a family and prepare for the celebration of Christ's birth. Seemed ironic to be doing those two things simultaneously.

Comforting things like food deliveries, visits from friends who could just sit with me, and people pointing me to Scripture, kept me vertical during those dark days. I also found that since I wasn't sleeping well at night, I almost always needed naps.

My denial of her being gone lasted until we went to Ellensburg a couple of days later. We basically went to retrieve Charley, who had been staying with her roommates. We quickly grabbed some things from her home that we needed for her memorial service. Some packages were there, which ended up being Christmas gifts and a small tree for her little home. I knew what was in the Amazon packages because we had just been discussing what Asher wanted for Christmas. It was his name that she drew from a hat just 2 weeks earlier. She had told me about getting a tree, but it hadn't arrived yet. My heart felt like it was in a thousand pieces as I sat on the floor in her room. I picked up a pile of her clothes, buried my face into them and just sobbed.

We had to go to the funeral home that day. The older kids, Brian, and I decided we didn't want to see her body. We wanted to remember her as she was that Thanksgiving of 2018. The funeral director was trying to persuade me to see her body. At one point he said "Sonya, I feel like you really want to see her body. Grief will be so much harder if you choose not to have this final goodbye. I sometimes see people in the grocery store six months later and they regret that they didn't view their loved ones." I understand his motive as I'm sure there are people who have regretted whatever decision they had to make under extreme duress. But to this day, I'm thankful for the decision we made. I remember her lively and laughing. Not lying cold in a coffin. It was an emotionally exhausting day for sure.

The following days were spent planning her memorial service. As a family we decided to have her cremated. Ironically, Mackenzie said that she had mentioned that one time to her, that she would rather be cremated than have an expensive casket. Always the minimalist. We met with our pastor and the pastor of the church that was allowing us to use their building. We picked songs and wrote memorials. All the kids needed new clothes. It was so mentally and physically draining.

In those first few days it felt like the world should stop. Our other kids should be angels. Why are they fighting again? Don't they know I need them out of my grieving space? Grieving parents should have bereavement leave from life. BUT, it does not work that way. Life goes on. Kids disobey. Teenagers fail classes and wreck the car. People post "mom and daughter" pictures on social media. Valued team members quit and add more stress to the husband's job. You get the picture.

I just longed for time to read, pray, be quiet, be loud, mourn, cry, scream, walk, run, look at photos, and try to understand and embrace my new reality. I had a huge desire to get on an airplane and go sit on a beach somewhere...alone. But life had to go on and it felt like I was dragging myself through a pit of mud each day.

In the exhaustion of the early grief, I learned a new lesson on grace. Well-meaning people will say the darndest things. To be clear, I have NO memory of which person said what. But the unhelpful comments stand out in my mind. Maybe I could provide a helpful list of what to say and what NOT to say, at least based on my own experience. I know everyone processes words differently, so this is strictly my experience.

Please, for the love of the family, don't ever ask details about the death in the rawness of grief. I had one person say, "Wasn't that why she got Charley? Why didn't Charley do anything?" That's like someone dying in a car crash and saying, "Well, was she wearing a seatbelt?" Maybe an alternative would be to say, "I'm here for you if and when you're ready to share."

"I know how you feel" became a phrase that made me cringe. Again, I want to emphasize that these comments are well-meaning from people with hearts of gold. But when someone would say these things, I wanted to scream, "NO! YOU DON'T KNOW HOW I FEEL! Please don't compare the death of your grandpa or a friend to me losing my DAUGHTER!" Grandparents are *supposed* to die. Friends will get sick. Children are not supposed to go before their parents. There is just nothing right about it. A better choice is simply to not even try to relate or compare anything you've been through to my grief. Maybe later in the course of the healing, but not in the rawness. It's hard to process your own grief, so being invited to see it through someone else's lens is simply too difficult in the early days of loss.

"God will never give you more than you can handle." This is a lie from hell. This has probably become one of my most despised cliches. God will absolutely give us more than we can handle. Otherwise, why would we need Him? I think a better way to say this is, "God will get you through it even when it seems like it might be the end of you."

"She's in a better place." Hmmmm. I kinda liked having her here. I hope she is! Otherwise what's the point to this life! An alternative to saying this would be....not saying it!

On the flip side I had so many encouraging words said to me! Having people tell me they're praying for our family, people doing practical things like bringing meals, cleaning our house, or taking the little boys for play dates. Since Kayla passed close to Christmas, I had friends who shopped for me and brought gifts for the kids, knowing we weren't up to this task ourselves. It was amazing to see the body of Christ be the hands and feet of Jesus to our family.

2 Corinthians 5:6-9 "So we are always of good courage. We know that while we are at home in the body we are away from the Lord, for we walk by faith, not by sight. Yes, we are of good courage, and we would rather be away from the body and at home with the Lord. So whether we are at home or away, we make it our aim to please Him." This verse gives me so much hope! It's natural as a Christ follower to long to be with Him. And that is where Kayla is. Until I am with Him, I will do my best to live to please Him.

I have a blog, https://sonyabonar.wordpress.com (Graced Mom), which I don't frequent often, but this was a post of mine that includes more scripture that encouraged me, and still does to this day.

Grief Has Entered
(written January 31, 2019)

Today marks eight weeks since our beloved eldest daughter (and child) went to the arms of Jesus. I'm not sure anyone can ever be prepared for the worst news of their life. I suppose there are worse things, but right now I can think of none. My emotions go from sadness to anger to disbelief in a matter of minutes.

I've been writing down some thoughts on grief and how it is affecting me. People have said in the past, "Grief comes in waves." I cannot think of a better explanation. The first few weeks the waves were constant. I could not even think of her name without breaking down. I couldn't pick up an article of her clothing, or read anything she had written. It was like I was never going to be able to walk, sleep, or live again.

113

But, life has to continue.

Pretty soon after the news, our focus turned into creating a beautiful memorial service, which I believe it was. Going through pictures, collecting memorabilia, anticipating family visiting, it all kept my mind moving. Then, Bam! It was over. Family left, memorabilia put back in boxes, ironed clothing hung on hangers in the closet.

Since then the waves are still present. But, they are less expected. Here are some examples:

Sitting in church, and on the big screen you find out your church is having a celebration. The date is her birthday.

Looking at your seven-year-old while he's looking at your phone. "Why does it say Kayla is in our house? I thought she was in heaven."

Riding in the car and a song comes on that she loved.

You get the picture. I continue to go (run) to Scripture to get my Comfort, Guidance, Healing (even though it feels like not much has taken place). I'd like to share some of those Words that have been breathed by God, and have kept me "walking without fainting." (Isaiah 40:31)

For comfort in knowing He is with me and will never leave me:

Isaiah 43:1-3 "But now says the Lord, he who created you, O Jacob, he who formed you, O Israel: Fear not, for I have redeemed you; I have called you by name, you are mine. When you pass through the waters, I will be with you; and through the rivers, they shall not overwhelm you; when you walk through fire you shall not be burned, and the flame shall not consume you. For I am the Lord your God, the Holy one of Israel, your Savior."

Isaiah 41:10 "Fear not, for I am with you; be not dismayed, for I am your God; I will strengthen you, I will help you, I will uphold you with my righteous right hand."

I could copy volumes of scripture for this topic. HE WILL NEVER LEAVE ME.

For the hope I have, knowing where Kayla is:

1 Thessalonians 4:13-14 "But we do not want you to be uninformed, brothers, about those who are asleep, that you may not grieve as others do who have no HOPE. For since we believe that Jesus died and rose again, even so, through Jesus, God will bring with Him those who have fallen asleep."

Kayla is with our Heavenly Father, perfect and whole.

For the hope I have, knowing where all of His people (including me) will be:

1 Thessalonians 4:15-18 "For this we declare to you by a word from the Lord, that we who are alive, who are left until the coming of the Lord, will not precede those who have fallen asleep. For the Lord Himself will descend from heaven with a cry of command, with the voice of an archangel, and with the sound of the trumpet of God. And the dead in Christ will rise first. Then we who are alive, who are left, will be caught up together with them in the clouds to meet the Lord in the air, and so we will always be with the Lord. Therefore ENCOURAGE one another with these words."

Talk about encouragement! Even if I don't die and meet Jesus before He comes again, I will be going to Him forever. These words from Paul, breathed by God, are such a lifter of my soul.

Again, there are so many scriptures that speak of this, but I'm trying to keep my readers awake. Ha!

For the hope in knowing my suffering is not wasted:

2 Corinthians 4:17-18 "For this light momentary afflic-tion is preparing for us an eternal weight of glory beyond all comparison, as we look not to the things that are seen but to the things that are unseen. For the things that are seen are tran-sient, but the things that are unseen are eternal."

2 Corinthians 1:3-5 "Blessed be the God and Father of our Lord Jesus Christ, the Father of mercies and God of all comfort, who comforts us in all our affliction, so that we may be able to comfort those who are in any affliction, with the comfort with which we ourselves are comforted by God. For as we share abundantly in Christ's sufferings, so through Christ we share abundantly in comfort too."

Matthew 5:4 "Blessed are those who mourn, for they shall be comforted."

Hope in knowing this is our temporary home here on earth:

As hard as it is to swallow some days, these afflictions are momentary. My life is just a mist that appears for a little time and then vanishes (James 4:14) This helps me to have an eter-nal perspective of why I'm suffering. And there is a promise that I can comfort others because of my own suffering.

2 Corinthians 5:1-2 "For we know that if the tent that is our earthly home is destroyed, we have a building from God, a house not made with hands, eternal in the heavens. For in this tent we groan, longing to put on our heavenly dwelling."

Philippians 1:21-23 "For to me to live is Christ, and to die is gain. If I am to live in the flesh, that means fruitful labor for me. Yet which I shall choose I cannot tell. I am hard pressed between the two. My desire is to depart and be with Christ, for that is far better."

I'd like to end with a verse that again, I have gone back to numerous times. It's so counterintuitive to our earthly minds and bodies, but it's spoken through Peter. 1 Peter 4:12-13 "Beloved, do not be surprised at the fiery trial when it comes upon you to test you, as though something strange were happening to you. But rejoice insofar as you share Christ's sufferings, that you may also rejoice and be glad when His glory is revealed."

Is my joy and hope always seen outwardly as I cry and throw laundry baskets across the room when I'm feeling angry? Is it seen when I'm running and tears are rolling down my face? Is it seen when I'm grumpy to my other children because I just can't do life that day? Definitely not. But I pray for grace from God and from other humans. And I hope that through this suffering I can exhibit the perpetual joy we are to have, even in the face of suffering.

Blessings, Sonya

I'd like to insert a blog about suffering and healthy responses. This was written after Kayla had been hospitalized in 2014, but I think it's relevant to this part of our story. Many things she said reflect my own experience after her death.

Before Opening Your Mouth
(blog by Kayla, April 2015)

"These past couple of days, I've had some really great conversations with people about the healing process and how difficult it is to be an individual struggling with a disability. Emotional healing, physical healing, the whole spectrum.

117

I'm not sure why it didn't hit me before, but most people are unable to provide adequate comfort and use discernment around people, such as myself, who have undergone serious emotional or physical trauma. This shouldn't come as surprising.

Although we—me and you—talk openly about trials and tribulations of all kinds, when it comes to being affirming and empathetic, the discussion ends. An excuse I've heard for not practicing affirmation and empathy is that some people cannot understand because they haven't gone through the exact same experience. While it would be great if we could all relate this way, that would only mean more people suffering. I wouldn't wish that on anyone.

After I returned home from the ICU in November (2014) I was struggling with borderline PTSD and severe anxiety and depression. The plethora of questions and promptings from friends and family that encouraged me to rehash the serious and unfortunate events was not something I was ready for. In fact, it's been five months now and only recently have I been emotionally prepared. Nonetheless, I answered the questions, but didn't realize later on that re-visiting this trauma was horrible for emotional healing.

I'm sharing this with the hope that you will read and hopefully think more seriously about how to approach a friend or family member whose physical and mental health is in a shaky place. I want my experiences to become teachable lessons that I can share with others through my spoken and written word.

Do Not Say:
1. God has a plan

2. *Jesus loves you, therefore, you have no reason to be depressed. Depression is sinful.*
3. *You're such a fighter!*

When I was hospitalized, I felt like my life was falling apart. It DID fall apart. When my plans for school, work, and relationships fell apart in a matter of twenty-four hours, I did NOT feel comforted or encouraged by the phrase "God has a plan." I didn't disown God by having these feelings.

Depression is a mental disorder. The many stigmas Christians have attached to the word "depression" and "anxiety" are wrong and the result has been a lack of healthy discussion about the issue. In the hospital, intubated, and then in a wheelchair, I found myself crying about my situation. I did not feel strong. I didn't feel worthy of praise for merely surviving a life-threatening event.

Don't get me wrong. I'm so thankful for my friends and family who helped keep me standing these past few months and I'm not disqualifying anything they said to me. If you read this and thought "oops I said that to her," it's OK. No long-term damage was made. My goal with this blog post is to promote better conversations, not idle ones that weren't my favorite.

Do Say:
1. *Nothing. Zip. Zilch.*
2. *I'm sorry you feel this way. What can I say or do (if anything) that would make this better?*
3. *I don't know what you're going through and I'm not going to pretend I do. Forgive me for anything that comes off as insensitive. If you feel like talking, please*

> *help me understand your situation more fully so I can better serve you and help you with this healing process.*
>
> *This may sound weird, but there have been many times when I asked people like my sister or my mom to simply sit with me. I said, "If I feel like talking, I'll speak up, but for now your presence is enough." Sometimes it is that simple. Instead of assuming you know the right words or actions, ask! What can I say or do? Another "do not say" would be, "I know how you feel." No you don't. Everyone is unique and so are their issues.*
>
> *Lastly, nobody likes a heart-breaker. Don't pretend to care and then leave. Let's try and be better supporters of our friends and family who are struggling! Kayla"*

Kayla was writing this from a different perspective. Hers was one of what people should or shouldn't say during recovery. Therefore, one thing I would disagree with in this post is not saying anything. Sometimes people will mention something about Kayla, or ask me how I'm doing and I start crying. Then they say, "Oh I knew I shouldn't have said anything. "No no no! Absolutely say something! I came across this quote that resonated with me. "If you know someone who has lost a very important person in their life and you're afraid to mention them because you may make them sad by reminding them that they died—you're not reminding them, they didn't forget that they died. What you're reminding them of is that you remembered they lived. And that is a great, great gift."

CHAPTER 15

The Memorial

Kayla's memorial service took place on December 15, 2018, just nine days after her passing. We had asked our previous church that had a big sanctuary if we could hold the service there. They were so generous to us.

We had a team who handled the food, a team who offered to decorate, family members from out of state helping with the tables and dressing the boys. Everything came together so nicely, which helps in the grief. Charley managed to jump on the counter and eat a bunch of muffins right before we left for the service. We even had a team to help with her if she needed to "excuse herself" during the service!

That afternoon over 300 people came to honor Kayla's life. Brian, Isaac, Mason, Mackenzie, and Riley all got up in front of the congregation and said a tribute. I was so incredibly proud of all of them. Isaac was the first sibling to go up on stage, and he gave such a beautiful tribute to Kayla.

> *"Hello, thank you everyone for coming out and celebrating Kayla's life with us. For those of you who don't know, I'm Isaac, the oldest of Kayla's many, many little brothers.*
>
> *I admired Kayla. She wasn't a person to sit idly by. Kayla applied herself to every aspect of her life, whether it was at church, school, or work. Kayla was an achiever. She was the only person I know who could listen to a podcast, crochet a scarf, read a book, and devour an entire bowl of popcorn*

simultaneously. She wasn't a quiet person. Kayla was someone who would tell you everything that was going on in her life, sometimes even if you didn't ask. Kayla wasn't shy about sharing her opinions and beliefs with others, even if they were complete strangers. She wasn't a person who was defined by her problems. Kayla lived every day to the fullest. She never complained about her health or let her issues stop her from living. Despite everything she dealt with daily, Kayla was happy. She wasn't a person who worried about what tomorrow will bring. She found peace in her writing, her friends, her family, and God. She was confident. Kayla would want us to find peace in her passing, however difficult it is to understand. She wasn't an average person. Kayla was a compassionate server, an inspiring writer, and an enthusiastic learner.

But the thing that I'll miss most about Kayla, is that she was my older sister. I know I will see her again, and that day cannot come soon enough. 1 Corinthians 15:50 says 'I declare to you, brothers and sisters, that flesh and blood cannot inherit the kingdom of God, nor does the perishable inherit the imperishable' Thank you."

After those heartfelt words from the oldest of her brothers, Mason took the stage.

"Hi, I'm Mason, the second oldest of Kayla's brothers. One of my favorite memories with Kayla were the days that we spent snowboarding and skiing together as a family. Whether it was night skiing at Stevens after school, or spending a long weekend at Whistler, these outings were always a way for us to connect and spend time with each other amidst the craziness

of our busy lives. While Isaac, Mackenzie, and I tend to move quickly down the hill, seeing who could finish the run first, Kayla always preferred to take her time. Always assuring us that she'd meet up with us shortly, she'd make wide and slow turns the entire way down the mountain, putting thought into every move and executing them with precision and care. Eventually, she'd meet up with us at the bottom of the hill, and we'd ride up with her for another run.

Kayla didn't look at life as a race or something to rush. Kayla spent her time on this earth at her own pace and on her own time, something I'll always admire greatly about her. She walked through life with strength and perseverance, and just like on the mountain, she made each move with care. Regardless of how long it took her or if she fell down a few times on the way, she always got back up and she always knew that we'd be there waiting for her and ready to take on another run.

On top of being an amazing sister, I'll always admire Kayla for her strength, resilience, and I'll never forget her contagious obnoxious laugh. I've been struggling to come up with the words to say, so I had Kayla help me a little bit. In a 2016 blog post about suffering, she wrote, 'I have known suffering and I have witnessed the suffering of others. And I will tell you this. None of it makes sense. I could spend a lifetime trying to untangle this mystery, but that would be a waste of time. I'd rather spend it learning how to love people better.' And that's exactly what she did. Thank you."

At this point in the service, I didn't think I could hear anymore about how my children were hurting, missing their older sister, yet probably still in shock that she was gone. Mackenzie, as the only sister of Kayla, had intimate and unique memories with her. These were her words.

> *"Good afternoon. I want to extend my deepest gratitude for everyone that is here to share in what Kayla would have wanted to be a celebration of life. Kayla was the oldest sister of Isaac, myself, Mason, Luke, Riley, Asher, and Elias. She took on this role, the role of being the oldest, quite seriously, especially when we would play house in our backyard as four apparent orphans. She acted like a little mother to me and my siblings as well as a few of the neighbor kids.*
>
> *Beyond having the responsibility of being the oldest sibling, she was my only sister. She took on this role quite beautifully. Kayla was my built-in best friend, my confidante, and my comrade amongst the many brothers. She was always there to celebrate with me in joyful moments and also to cry with me in sorrowful seasons.*
>
> *Kayla had an intuition that allowed her to connect on a deeper level than just any superficial relationship. She felt so deeply for people and carried the hurt of the world on her shoulders. I remember this one day in particular, that I was caught up in the rumble and tumble of my brothers, and I was crying about what any nine-year-old had to be crying about. Kayla gently invited me into her room, where she had laid out an outfit, with a skirt for each of us, and she had assembled china dishes for us to have our own tea party. Initially, I was irritated because I didn't like to wear anything other than my usual pair of basketball shorts and T-shirt, but little did I know that she was nurturing a relationship that I never knew I needed.*

Having tea with my sister that one afternoon, led to many more conversations about faith, life, and relationships as we got older. It led to many coffee dates as well, because we both came to know that we didn't like tea. Quite honestly, I don't think I would be who I am today without my sister, Kayla, and I'm not just talking about the unibrow I'd have if it wasn't for Kayla telling me to wax my eyebrows, or the tangled hair I'd have if she didn't give my mom the product review of the shampoo she called "hairball easiness", also known as Herbal Essence.

Kayla saw me for who I was and taught me to treat others the same. The truth is, it's not about our outward appearance, but instead the inner self. Kayla exemplified a woman of Christ through her tender heart and outspoken faith. In 1 Peter 3:4, it says, 'But let your adorning be the hidden person of the heart with the imperishable beauty of a gentle and quiet spirit, which in God's sight is very precious.' Kayla's instinctive nature and beauty blossomed from the trust she put in Jesus Christ as her Saviour.

It's my new reality that my sister is no longer living on this side of eternity, but she used her time wisely and gave me the most beautiful gift of sisterhood. These past couple of days I've been reminiscing memories of my sister, and I remember the day before my birthday this year when Kayla and I rode down to Oregon to meet family. I remember it so clearly. We were just before the Lewis and Clark Bridge and there was a railroad crossing that had backed up traffic for probably an hour. In the moment I was very impatient and hungry for more than the small box of raspberries Kayla had packed away in her purse, not thinking to refrigerate them. As impatient as I felt in that moment, I now realize that it was a whole extra hour that

> *God gave me to spend with my sister. And I thought about how important it is for us to take hold of every moment because in James 4:14 it says, 'Yet you do not know what tomorrow will bring, what is your life? For we are a mist that appears for a little time and then vanishes.' And in Isaiah 40:7-8 it says, 'The grass withers, the flower fades when the breath of the Lord blows on it; surely the people are grass. The grass withers, the flower fades, but the Word of our God will stand forever.' We can rest assured in the hope of salvation because the Word of God will never fade."*

Riley took the stage, and for a nine-year-old, did an awesome job reading a prayer that Kayla had said as a three-year-old. I was humbled by his ability to carry himself, to read so clearly, and to share his own childlike wisdom with Scripture.

> *"Hello, my name is Riley. I am Kayla's nine-year-old brother, and I would like to read a prayer that was said by my sister and written down by our Great Aunt, Lela Pettit. 'A Different Prayer,' by Lela Pettit. Lela is Kayla's great-aunt. Dale is her husband. It was written October 1998, shortly after Sonya told her this story:*
>
> *'..And God, please be with Dale's mom, Jean, because she is sick. Help her not to be sick anymore.' These words were the nightly prayer of my three-year-old great-niece, Kayla. During the four months my husband's mother was in the hospital fighting cancer, Kayla's mom, Sonya, told me that they would miss bedtime prayers occasionally as a family, but Kayla never forgot to pray without being reminded.*
>
> *Though she is only three, just watching her process things, it is obvious that she is a deep thinker beyond her years. When she*

*hears family or friends tell stories about times prior to her time,
she often interrupts with, 'Where was I?' Sonya has explained
to her that she was in heaven with God before she was born.
In fact, it's Biblical. Jeremiah 1:5, 'Before I formed you in the
womb, I knew you. Before you were born, I set you apart. I
appointed you as a prophet to the nations.'*

*Jean's life was the Catholic Church and her family. As a
result, her entire life was spent in constant Christ-like, selfless
devotion to her family. She loved children. She had nine of her
own and twelve grandchildren—and gave all of herself to each
one of them.*

*One night after Jean had died, Sonya went into Kayla's
room to read to her and begin the nightly ritual of preparing
for bed. That night Kayla was already sitting on her bed and
told her mom that she had just said a prayer for Dale's mom,
Jean. Sonya had to tell her the sad news and try to explain
that Jean had gone to heaven and that she wasn't sick anymore.
Without hesitation, Kayla said, 'Then I need to pray a different prayer.' In childlike faith, this was her prayer, 'Dear God,
help Dale understand that his mom is in heaven and she won't
be sick anymore. And I hope Jean has fun playing with all the
babies that haven't been born yet.'*

*I have a verse I would like to share, Matthew 8:17, 'This
was to fulfill what was spoken by the prophet Isaiah. 'He took
our illnesses and bore our diseases.' I think God healed them
in a different way. He called them home and healed their diseases. Thanks."*

When we were planning the service, I was actually very surprised that Brian wanted to speak. I know for me, I was too fragile

and devastated. I couldn't even think of what I would say. I was very blessed by his words.

"Isaac told me 'I got this,' so I'm gonna try. I'll need your help. As Isaac said, welcome to all who have come here today, from near and far, as well as some of those who are maybe Facebooking live, to join us in remembering and celebrating Kayla.

In the midst of a week that is unimaginable to think of as a parent, Sonya and I were searching for the words of how to best honor Kayla and share with you about her story. Kayla was a big sister, a daughter, a cousin, a granddaughter, a niece, a friend, and a COUG. She was also a voracious reader and a journalist who wrote a lot. We have boxes of journals that will serve as a way for Sonya and I and her siblings to connect with her for a long time.

As the anxiety was building this week, and I was asking myself how we will tell her story, we looked to some of her own words to give a glimpse into her heart and her daily walks. This is from her blog, Coffee Shop Talk, March 2014. 'Hope is hard. It's a fact of life. But hope is also beautiful. It means we are choosing to believe that there is, indeed, a light at the end of a very dark tunnel. And that, my friend, is no easy feat. Hope is counting on and clinging to what we cannot see. Hope is what we grab hold of as we're searching for peace in the middle of a war. Hope is not always comforting, but sometimes it's all we have. If hope were a person, I wonder what he'd say or what he'd do. I'd like to believe that he'd take my hand and say, 'Here's my hand, you can squeeze it.' Hope would know that if I can't change my present circumstances, I'm better off knowing I don't need to endure the battle ahead alone. Faith and hope work closely together. Without faith, how could we hope? How else could we confidently say, 'Everything will work out.' Hope is the product of faith. C.S. Lewis once said that 'Faith is the art of holding on to things in spite of your changing moods and circumstances.' Sounds a lot like hope, doesn't it? Not everyone may believe in God, but it would take an incredible amount of convincing for someone to tell me they didn't have hope. We have hope in our friends, our family, our circumstances, and in tangible things. However, I've found the most beautiful sort of hope is that which can't be seen or heard or touched, but still believed in. Kayla. Hebrews 6:19 'We have this hope as an anchor for the soul, firm and secure.'

It's special being here today on a stage where Kayla first expressed her boldness as part of many youth productions, singing and laughing, and also getting baptized. All of these moments set her on a path. Kayla's heart for others stirred her at eight, to go on a mission trip to Alaska ministering to churches. As Tom mentioned, she traveled to Mexico to build homes and support children. Going to Haiti, though, in 2012, reaching and serving orphanages, transformed her heart greatly.

As parents, Sonya and I struggled constantly with the desire to hold her close to home and protect her, knowing full well her affliction was always lingering. Sonya and I were continually challenged in our faith to allow her to live out her hope of going on mission trips, going to school to achieve a degree, and working towards a career, living apart and in community in Ellensburg.

Kayla was the most fearless person I have ever known. We now know, looking back, if we did not trust and have hope, and let Kayla live out her faith, taking risks in light of her affliction, she never would have fulfilled God's plan for her life. Her last-ing impact would have looked much different, and lives, such as many are here today, would not have been changed. Kayla will live in the stories that will be shared amongst you and moving forward as well as in the writing she left with us and her siblings, boxes of journals, and a long reading list. I will miss the late-night conversations with her asking, 'Dad, how was your day?' Despite how hard her days could be, she was never asking, 'Why is life so hard?' or saying 'I wish things were different.' This was the beautiful quality about Kayla.

Our last time together was just a short three weeks ago at Thanksgiving. We're a Costco sized family so everything comes in bulk, including commotion with everyone's work and school schedules, plus four younger brothers. But we were together, and that's all that mattered to Sonya and I. Looking back, we shared some sweet, precious moments during those few days with Kayla, home from Ellensberg, and Isaac back from WSU. Go Cougs! I feel so blessed looking back as a dad, to have had a few moments alone with Kayla in the car. We were just talking about life stuff in the short term. With winter approaching she talked about getting back on the mountain slopes, something she had not experienced the last couple of years since her part-nership with Charley, her service dog. I've spent a lot of time on the mountains in the snow with our kids. I always appreciated long lift rides with them in the stillness of the falling snow, unplugged, and having soft conversations. From Snoqualmie, to Crystal, to Stevens, to Whistler, it was a passion of mine to have an activity we could enjoy, and snow was that arena. Kayla started snowboarding at an early age, but a few years ago at Whistler she tried skiing. In that time, in the car, over

Thanksgiving, she said to me, 'I wish I hadn't tried skiing, Dad, I really liked it.' Then she asked, 'Dad, I think I would like to try it again.' She was fearless and tenacious and full of hope in what she could accomplish.

We then briefly talked about bikes, and Kayla said she was thinking of getting a used bike with a pull behind carrier for Charley. Since she couldn't drive, Kayla often had long daily walks in solitude to and from work, to the store, to get groceries or other daily needs. In that moment, I was reminded that Kayla was undaunted by life and didn't ask why simple things were so hard. She was our hero of perseverance. When I look at this photo behind me, I'm reminded that Kayla was always looking up. She was always searching, both in obedience and with a curiosity for the big things God might have in store for her. But she also had the quality of focusing on the simple things that mattered to her. Our conversation ended with her saying, 'Dad, you know I can ride a bike really well.' She said it with such Kayla conviction. We laughed and I told her, 'You can do anything.'

Don't be heavy hearted today for Kayla. For she is with Christ and she pursued and fulfilled a beautiful life, courageously, gracefully, lovingly, and humbly, with rigor and selflessness. For this, Sonya, Isaac, Mason, Mackenzie, Luke, Riley, Asher, and Elias, are all at peace knowing her hope was in her salvation. Hebrews 11:1-3 tells us, 'wherever there is assurance of hope, there is faith, and faith is the full assurance of hope.' Thank you."

Photo credit: Luke White

The service was a beautiful tribute. I was so thankful to hear friends whom I had never met stand up and talk about how she had blessed their lives, or said something that was wise and comforting. It was another wonderful reminder of her maturity in Christ beyond her years. I'm so thankful for family that traveled from IL, TX, TN, NE, MT, AZ, and friends as far as IN and HI! We are a blessed family, and I continue to thank God that we had that special day of remembrance.

CHAPTER 16

Navigating a New Normal

The First Christmas

Christmas came whether we were ready or not. Christmas morning we were blessed with a full breakfast from one of the small groups at our church. We feasted, even though I don't think any of us had felt hunger in three weeks. All seven children were home on Christmas morning. We have a tradition in which each child draws a name. We call it their "special person" gift. When everyone was younger, we would take them all out individually to shop for their person. This usually included some kind of treat and some much needed quality time with mom and dad. As the older kids started driving, they did their own shopping. I'm still fortunate to be able to take the four youngest on their shopping trips.

After breakfast was the time for the special person's gift. We started with the youngest that year. Elias had Kayla's name. Just four days before she passed we had our special shopping trip. I took him to a place called "Country Village," which has since been torn down and replaced by housing. He decided to get her some Christmas ornaments because he had heard she had ordered a small tree. In fact, this small tree had come from Amazon and she never got to open it. We also went to the Brooks store and got her some new shoes. She was not good at buying things for herself, and her tennis shoes were on their last thread! Elias opened up the gifts for her and explained what each one was and why he chose it. We were all crying while he, in his innocent five-year-old voice, shared about his shopping trip. Asher then gave his special person their gift, and all the way up until it would have been Kayla's turn. I looked over at Asher and he had a look on his face of pure sadness, as he realized he was the only one left without a gift. He ran over to me, threw himself in my arms and sobbed. After he calmed down a little, I gave him the gifts that Kayla had bought. Just the night before she died, she told me she was still waiting on the gifts from Amazon, and they were in her house that day we went over to gather some things. He opened an Echo dot and a black watch. He had put both of those things on his Christmas list, and ironically, he had told Mason a couple of days prior that he had dreamed of receiving a black watch for Christmas. More crying and hugging, and we proceeded with the morning.

That afternoon, we went over to Brian's parents' house. This is another tradition we participate in every Christmas. Since they live locally, we spend the afternoons with them. To be honest, I don't remember much about that afternoon. I was pretty much in a daze of grief, all the while trying to be excited for the gifts we were opening.

We had been given an amazing meal to cook, prepared by another small group in our church. We had a roast, ham, two types of potatoes, green bean casserole, rolls, and pies. Again, not having to plan any meals that first Christmas was HUGE. So so grateful.

After we got the boys back home, I remember being so exhausted I could hardly stand up. Just the pure emotions of the day, not to mention Christmas is always exhausting for parents of young kids! While putting the boys to bed, Asher said, "Mom, thanks for a good Christmas. I know Kayla had a good one too." That made the day, as hard as it was, worth every second.

A New Year Rolls In

For the first part of 2019, I often went to bed wishing I could just wake up to a new day. Sleeping and resting seemed impossible. This was my journal entry from January 6, 2019:

"I slept horribly. I woke up at 3 a.m. with such physical pain missing my girl. I have to recite over and over again that she is free, she's with Jesus. 'Even the darkness is not dark to you.' Psalm 139:12"

One of my journal entries two months into the grief:

> *"Today the grief is unbearable. I cried at Elias' school, I cried in the garage, and I blame myself.*
>
> *I keep seeing her picture by the water, that was her newest Facebook profile picture. How long will I wake up and count the days since Kayla's passing? Could God forgive me if I drove into the guardrails? But I can't, too many people rely on me. I actually started to send Kayla a text today. Then I froze. I HATE THIS! I selfishly want her with me. I regret the times I was impatient with her neediness."*

Photo credit: Jake Green

Some might say I sounded suicidal. I didn't want to take my life, but I was certainly fine with meeting Christ any day. There's a difference between being suicidal and not caring if you die. I definitely didn't care for a few months.

The days all seemed to blur together those first weeks. Before I knew it, it was time for Kayla's birthday. I remember sitting in church about a month before her birthday. Suddenly, up on the big screen was an announcement, "February 10, Happy Birthday!" I immediately had to get up and leave the room. Our church plant was about to celebrate its first birthday on, you guessed it, Kayla's birthday. After church that day we were to have lunch and a cake.

As God would have it, the party for church had to be postponed. A huge snowstorm came through and many people were unable to get out on the roads. We got a message that some friends were having a potluck brunch at their house, and a lot of church friends would be there. So, we got up and got ready to go.

There were a lot of tears for me that day, seeing things that people wrote on social media, or sending texts. Late in the morning we arrived at our friends' house. We had a delicious meal, they built a bonfire and we sang worship songs, and the kids went sledding. It was actually a wonderful gift from God to be with a smaller crowd and to see the kids having fun again.

From several ladies, I received a gold necklace with a 'K', and a beautiful framed calligraphy piece from a friend. She took a quote of Kayla's and added scripture. It read:

You asked me to take the path less traveled, a narrow messy one
That leads to a beautiful destination.
Help me as I run this race.
Continue reminding me that the sun still shines by showing me

The shadows.
Kayla Bonar

When you pass through the waters, I will be with you
And through the rivers
They shall not overwhelm you.
When you walk through fire
You shall not be burned
And the flame shall not overcome.
Isaiah 43:2

The day had some laughable moments, some extremely sad moments, and some frustrating moments. When the women presented me with the gifts, I read it out loud (through tears) so that everyone in the room knew what it said. Then Elias said, "Well, that makes no sense!" We all had a good laugh—some needed relief from the sadness.

Our pastor and his wife also dropped by after the gathering with a beautiful variety of plants in a pot. We didn't know any Haitian dishes, but for dinner Kenzie made pancit (a Philipino dish) in honor of Kayla's love for overseas missions and her heart for the people.

Overall, it was a beautiful day. Having all the kids together is basically my desire for her birthdays. Inevitably, we end up sharing memories over tears and laughs.

Happy Heavenly Birthday

Time seemed to stand still and fly by at the same time. During the rest of 2019, it was "business as usual" with a 50 pound weight on my shoulders. Trudging through each day, but also having days of joy amidst the sorrow. Somehow, we survived and then it was December 6th again.

The day began with me crying. I had gone to Facebook. Big mistake. I wish I could obey the Lord and go to the Word first! God is still molding my habits. The first thing that popped up was the post that Mackenzie shared on Facebook.

> *"One year since my sister went to heaven. One year since my world felt like it stopped spinning. There is nothing that could have prepared me for this year of grief. The type that comes on unexpectedly when you're standing in the middle of the grocery store, when you hear a song on the radio, or when you shut the car door after a day at work. Though I wasn't prepared for these moments, God has sustained me by filling me with hope, peace, and comfort that only comes from Him.*
>
> *My mind is flooded with fond memories of the amazing sister, friend, and daughter Kayla embodied. When she first left for college, I thought I was left to despair with six brothers at home. Only to find out that she would accomplish her dream of becoming a journalist. And she would touch many lives along the way. She would continue to encourage me, love me, and challenge me— despite her own difficulties. Our late-night FaceTime calls and girl's weekends would become treasured and I would quickly learn that a sister is a friend like no other. And I am grateful for the gift of sisterhood that Kayla gave me.*

Even the most joyful moments of this year have been tainted with immense sadness that Kayla isn't here to celebrate.

But there is no greater joy than the joy she is experiencing with our Creator in heaven. "You make known to me the path of life; in your presence there is fullness of joy; at your right hand are pleasures forevermore."

Mackenzie's twin brother, Mason, wrote a beautiful post reflecting his own grief.

"I was told that grief would come in waves, at unexpected moments,

but nobody warned me of drowning, or the constant effort I would need to make to keep my head above the water I continue to tread.

are you there?

at 4 a.m. when I lie awake replaying conversations
when I get in my car and start crying out of nowhere
when I feel like I'm the only person in the world that feels this way,
isolated and alone,
are you there?
I was told that I would be reminded of you, even by the smallest things.
I feel you in the sunlight coming through the trees
I hear you in songs on the radio, you always loved to sing
I see you in the changing color of the sky in the evening
beautiful and serene
Are you there?
I know you are.

One year without our Kayla and it still doesn't feel real at times. The last year has been full of grieving and learning to find joy in the sad moments. I never thought a year could feel so long yet so fast at the same time. Today is a sad day, but Kayla's presence is strong. I feel blessed to have the precious memories I do with her. I feel lucky to have a sister who hasn't left my side, even when she's not here on earth.

Kayla didn't let sickness or other's opinions define her. She lived life the way she wanted despite her obstacles. She carried herself with strength and love in the most difficult seasons, what an inspiring way to live. ♥Mason"

We spent the day as a family, going to a few Christmas tree farms to find a tree. There were some laughs and some tears. We went out to dinner and bought a purple balloon to place in Kayla's place. We navigated the first heavenly birthday the best we knew how.

Purple has become our color. It's the color that represents epilepsy, and it happened to be Kayla's favorite color as well. Most of my gifts from friends and family now are purple—blankets, jewelry, and I treasure it all! Some of my family members keep one fingernail painted purple to remember her. I love some excerpts from this blog about the color purple.

P is for Purple
(blog by Kayla, April 2013)

"Today is "Purple For Epilepsy Day." I love purple. My favorite childhood classic book—Little Women by Louisa May Alcott—is bound with a purple cover. I have a purple

raincoat, purple bible, purple water-bottle, purple toothbrush, purple, purple, purple, purple..... I think you understand the picture. Only recently, within the past couple of years, did I actually connect the color purple with epilepsy. At this point I can imagine you are thinking, "So what?" So, I have epilepsy. I've thought about writing a post—or a few pages in my journal—for some time, but I didn't want to come off as someone looking for attention or be labeled 'epileptic.' Is it obvious yet I have a severe pride issue? OK, I thought so. (I'm so glad God blessed me with the gift of sarcasm, otherwise I'd be a mess.) Anyways, I put off writing about my epilepsy for purely selfish reasons. Then, I realized that there are easily a gazillion other people, NOT sharing their stories—whether health related or not—for exactly the same reasons. This is why I'm asking YOU to share your stories.

OK, hold the phone right there. A story or testimony doesn't have to be something heart-wrenching. I've seen too many people demean their own stories simply because they thought it wasn't "moving" or "shocking." Heck, the most relatable stories are in the form of "little" everyday problems. I.e.,

Person 1: You received a D on your Spanish test?

Person 2: Dude me too.

If you have struggled with serious issues in the past or are struggling currently, here is my message to you: YOU ARE NOT ALONE. That thought is a lie. Only you can make the choice to believe it. Keeping your fears and feelings bottled up is the worst decision you could possibly make. If you don't believe me, believe Dumbledore when he says "Numbing the pain for a while will make it worse when you finally feel it." Trust me, Albus Dumbledore doesn't lie.

I've had epilepsy for over 10 years. It's definitely a reality, but it doesn't define who I am. What defines me is how I respond to the ups and downs. The hospital visits, the sick days, and the days when I ask "Why me?" And then I look around me. I could be so much worse off. I have so many things to be thankful for. Best of all I love knowing that no matter what kind of situation God puts me in, it's only to refine me! We should bear these challenges—even something as insignificant as a Spanish test—knowing that there is definitely something to be learned so that next time, you can do better. If you think you can fight this battle on your own, good luck with that. I've tried and failed. It's easy to look strong on the outside and inwardly destroy yourself. When people tell you "Wow you are so strong!" Things begin going to your head. Society tells us it's not okay to be weak. I'd like you to consider otherwise.

Remember, there are always consequences for going against the grain. Humbleness isn't a trait valued by most. I don't know about you, but when people ask me how I'm doing, I enjoy testing their sincerity by telling them the flat-out truth. I may say "Well actually this week kinda sucked." I know people who I know are going through hell and still respond with "oh I'm doing just dandy." Sorry to break it to you, but nobody's perfect.

But he said to me, 'My grace is sufficient for you, for my power is made perfect in weakness. Therefore I will boast all the more gladly about my weaknesses, so that Christ's power may rest on me. That is why, for Christ's sake, I delight in weaknesses, in insults, in hardships, in persecutions, in difficulties. For when I am weak, then I am strong.' (2 Corinthians 12:9-10) Kayla"

CHAPTER 17

Suffering and Trials

When trying to understand suffering (or trials), I think it's imperative to distinguish between the purpose of suffering and the 'why' of suffering. The former can be understood by going to Scripture. The latter, in my opinion, may be different for each person, and often, never known. As a follower of Christ, I look to Romans 8:28, which reads "And we know that for those who love God, all things work together for good, for those who are called according to his purposes." There are no restrictions in this verse. All means all. If I am who I say I am in Christ, then I have to believe that the purpose of Kayla's death will result in good for me and glory for God. It goes against what our common sense says. Common sense says no human should have to lose a child, and how could any good come from it? Hence, why some people might deal with anger as part of their grief. Or perhaps they may deny there is God when something awful happens.

I believe another purpose for suffering is to gain opportunities to comfort others in their own suffering. In his letter to the church in Corinth, Paul writes, "Blessed be the God and Father of our Lord Jesus Christ, the Father of mercies and God of all comfort, who comforts us in our affliction, so that we may be able to comfort those who are in any affliction, with the comfort with which we ourselves are comforted by God. For as we share abundantly in Christ's sufferings, so through Christ we share abundantly in comfort too." 2 Corinthians 1:3-5. I have been able to share the pain of other mothers going through the loss of a child. I pray that I can continue to point the grieving to the One who is the Ultimate Comfort.

Could it be possible that a purpose of suffering is to teach us to rejoice? We can rejoice knowing that He will be glorified through our suffering, even when that feels impossible. Back to Paul (can you tell I like him?), he writes in his letter to the Romans about this. "Therefore, since we have been justified by faith, we have peace with God through our Lord Jesus Christ. Through him we have also obtained access by faith into this grace in which we stand, and we rejoice in hope of the glory of God. More than that, we rejoice in our sufferings, knowing that suffering produces endurance, and endurance produces character, and character produces hope, and hope does not put us to shame, because God's love has been poured into our hearts through the Holy Spirit who has been given to us." Romans 5:1-5. I am promised to receive endurance, character and hope! Those are pretty lofty promises! Earlier in Chapter 8, he writes, "For I consider that the sufferings of this present time are not worth comparing with the glory that is to be revealed to us." Roman 8:18. That should give the suffering something to rejoice over. Did I say that would be easy? No, but two years later I can say it is easier to think of the glory coming for eternity. When I think of a rope that can go around the world a million times, and my life is the first inch of that rope, eternity sounds like something to rejoice about!

Also, I must understand and accept that God allows a believer to face trials and suffering. However, the promise of Romans 8 is that he will also allow GOOD to come from it. It is our job to allow the grace of Jesus Christ and the Holy Spirit to work. I didn't allow this for a while, as I was dealing with grief in a worldly way while trying to weave God into it. I can tell you, that process does NOT work.

In my own experience, I discover some 'whys' to my suffering. My suffering has led to complete dependence on the Lord. There is nothing in the world that can heal a broken heart. Not alcohol, not TV, not friends, and not even the church. Christ following friends are critical, but not the answer.

Another 'why' Scripture reveals, points me towards my eternal life with Christ. Before Kayla's death, I always believed I would go to heaven, but I didn't think much about it. I never ever thought about the rapture. I thought Revelation was confusing and had never been taught much about it. God put people in my life that directed me towards studying prophecy. It is approximately one third of the bible, but yet, one third of the sermons I've heard are not directed to prophecy. In the book of John, Jesus is telling his disciples He will come again. "Let not your hearts be troubled. Believe in God; believe also in me. In my Father's house are many rooms. If it were not so, would I have told you that I go to prepare a place for you? And if I go to prepare a place for you, I will come again and take you to myself, that where I am you may be also." How awesome is this? I've read this passage dozens of times, but it took on a new meaning to me after I knew Kayla was there. I wonder what her room looks like!

A third 'why' that is taking place is pruning. God has used this loss to prune some sin out of my life. The more I'm in the Word, the more He shows me what areas I need to work on with His help. In John 15, Jesus says, "I am the true vine, and my Father is the vine-dresser. Every branch that does not bear fruit he takes away, and every branch that does bear fruit he prunes, that it may bear more fruit." The word 'abide' appears in this chapter around twenty-three times. If we are abiding in Him, or accepting His ways and with His help, living that way, He will show us areas in our lives that are not honoring Him. Here are some thoughts from a blog by Kayla. Again, her spiritual maturity and insight continue to amaze me.

"Faith and Healing"
(blog post by Kayla, November 2016)

"I asked myself the question that I've been wrestling with for most of my life: why do bad things happen to good people? Some people have this twisted view that Christians or morally good people have somehow earned the right to a better and easier life. I can see where they're coming from, it seems logical. However, the blessing of suffering isn't less suffering. It's humility. A deep dependence on the One who carries me in the midst of my suffering.

Bad things happen to the best of us. Suffering can be redeemed by using our experiences to empathize with each other. Suffering is the result of sin but that doesn't mean we can't live like we don't have a healer. Kayla"

CHAPTER 18

Honoring and Healing

After Kayla went to be with the Lord, we, as a family, wanted to find ways to keep her Legacy alive. We pondered different ideas, and came up with the idea of a scholarship at WSU. After some research and contacting some people in the office, we decided on an Endowment. If we reach a goal of $25,000, the Endowment will go on forever as the money is invested. If we keep raising money, the amount of the scholarship will increase slowly. As of now, we are at the goal! The document is being written up, and we will then sign the papers. At that time, the money will be invested, and as soon as we can give $1,000 to a student, it will begin. The student to receive the scholarship must meet one or more of the following criteria: have an interest in rural journalism, participate in the WSU Student Access Center, have demonstrated community service involvement, and maintain a minimum GPA of 2.5, and preference for a woman recipient. The Access Center is a place for students to get help with special needs they may have due to a disability. Kayla needed this service in case she missed a class because of a seizure, needed extra time on a test, or needed a different environment to take a test. I'm thankful for the work these people do for the students of WSU.

My daughter and I have formed a group called 'Kilometers for Kayla'. A few months after she died, we did a run in her honor. Mackenzie had shirts made that said 'Kilometers for Kayla' on the front in purple. On the back is 2 Timothy 4:7, "I have fought the good fight, I have finished the race, I have kept the faith."

For my 50th birthday in September 2020, we broke the gathering rules and hosted a run to celebrate my birthday and to raise money for her Endowment. Instead of an entry fee, we asked people to donate $50 to her Endowment fund. We had around 30 people show up that morning. We even received pictures from friends around the country wearing their Kayla shirts during their virtual 5K. It was amazing, and I'm so thankful for the friends and family that participated. We also had people contribute who weren't even running! That day we received over $1,000 in donations to her fund. If you are interested in contributing to Kayla's Endowment, here is the link: https://bit.ly/30hZrdG

The first few months after Kayla's death I floundered in my grief. Brian and I had a couple of helpful counseling sessions. I found a grief counselor that was helpful for a time. I remembered seeing a flyer for a program called 'Griefshare.' I googled it in the spring after she passed. I found a group that was to start in the Fall of 2019. Brian and I registered with a church I was familiar with.

I remember walking in that first meeting. Any kind of social gathering, church service, or Bible study felt so heavy. I wasn't sure what to expect. I had never met our amazing leaders, Steve and Sally. As I entered in with Brian, I felt a sense of peace. There's something about knowing you're not alone anymore. The people in that room were each on their own grief journey, and it was both comforting and heavy to hear each of their stories.

I completed two sessions of Griefshare—once with Brian and Mackenzie, and the second by myself. Griefshare is a three component program. Through discussions, DVD lessons, and questions in the workbook, I learned that many of the feelings and emotions I had and continue to have are completely normal. Many times I had to force myself to do the homework, but it was always beneficial.

I remember someone saying that healing is moving forward if you can begin to feel gratefulness for that person and the time you had with them, instead of feeling intense pain. As I write this, it has been over two years since Kayla went to be with the Lord. I don't think the pain will ever go away fully, but it isn't as intense on a daily basis as it was for so long. I have deep gratitude to the Lord for Him placing Kayla in my life and choosing me to be her mother. I'd like to share something Kayla wrote in a blog after returning from Haiti. I'm so often still in awe of the depth of her insights and her relationship with the Lord.

> *"Gratitude turns what we have into enough, and more. It turns denial into acceptance, chaos into order, confusion into clarity...it makes sense of our past, brings peace for today, and creates a vision for tomorrow."*

When I purposefully choose to be grateful for my past, present and future, my heart feels right, and I think it pleases the Lord! In fact, another part of my healing has been my gratitude journal.

Six months to the day after Kayla passed, the daughter of her former editor in Ellensburg passed away. This little girl had also battled a neurological disorder, but it was much more severe than anything Kayla had dealt with. I asked my friend if she would make the trip over the mountain to Ellensburg and attend the memorial with me. I knew it would be an emotional time, and I wanted someone there with me. Brian graciously stayed home with the kids. The memorial was very sweet. I'm unsure right now of her exact age, but she was less than nine years old.

After the memorial, my friend and I decided to walk around downtown and frequent some of the shops that Kayla and I, or Mackenzie, Kayla, and I had visited. Ellensburg really is a quaint little town with a lot of character. We roamed through a bookstore, a clothing store, and were drawn into a gift shop. We were looking at some little leather-bound journals. My friend said, "I want to buy this for you because it reminds me of Kayla." I told her we should both buy one and begin gratefulness journals. That was a year and a half ago. We are now on our third or fourth journal! Our goal is to write down at least three things each day that we are grateful for, take a screenshot, and send it to one another.

As a fallen human, there are some days where I just sit and stare at the page after putting everyone to bed. Some days I feel like all

I do is clean up messes, discipline boys, and break up wrestling matches. But there is ALWAYS something to be grateful for! Most importantly is the fact that the Lord is full of mercy.

Healing from losing a child probably never completely takes place. With finding support groups, being grateful, and surrounding oneself with truth, I believe the Hope that we have pulls us out of the pit.

CHAPTER 19

THE GOSPEL IS FOR EVERYONE

When I first started thinking about writing my story, I was excited to have a chance to share the gospel. Although it may just be close friends and family who read this, my prayer is that if one life can be brought to Christ, this work is worth it. Writing is not easy! I will elaborate more on that shortly!

If you don't know what I mean by the word gospel, it means "good news." It's the amazing, almost unbelievable news that we can be saved from our sins and an eternity separated from the Lord, in a place known as hell. Jesus Christ came to earth as an infant, God incarnate, and lived among people as the only perfect human being. He taught for three years, bringing many to Himself, but also rejected by many. At the end of his teaching, he was crucified on the cross. Through the blood of Christ, we are justified from our sin. Jesus took all of God's Wrath upon Himself on that cross. We don't have to experience the judgement of our sin or God's Wrath because Christ took all of it for us. His blood is the propitiation for our sin.

Many might say, "My life is fine. I am a good person. I don't really have any sin in my life. I don't need God." I can see why someone might say this. However, if you have never accepted Jesus as your Lord and Savior, you haven't yet experienced the joy and peace that this brings. No other religion on the planet gives eternal life through grace alone, not by works. Ephesians 2:8-9 assures us, 'For by grace you have been saved through faith. And this is not your

153

own doing; it is the gift of God, not a result of works, so that no one may boast.'

One pastor that I listen to frequently ends all of his prophecy updates with the gospel. He breaks it down into the ABCs of Salvation.

'A' stands for admit. All of us are sinners. Just being a "good person" isn't good enough. No one can do enough good deeds in their lifetime and go to heaven without admitting sin and most importantly, repenting. We can all admit sin and then go on living the same life. Until we repent, our hearts can't experience real change. So, whether you think so or not, you're a sinner! Let's back that up with scripture. In Romans, Paul writes, "none is righteous, no, not one; no one understands, no one seeks for God." Romans 3:10-11. In context, he is saying that the Jew and the Gentile are both sinners and guilty before God. In a nutshell, that means EVERYONE. The absolute first step in becoming a follower of Christ is admitting you're a sinner and repenting, meaning you do not wish to sin anymore. Will you still sin? Yes. There has only been one non-sinner on the earth, and that is Jesus Christ. What is the cost of sin without saving grace? Romans 6:23, Paul writes "For the wages of sin is death, but the free gift of God is eternal life in Christ Jesus our Lord." This sounds like bad news. (the wages of sin is death). But, it's really good news (the gift of God is eternal life). Personally, I think the hardest part of becoming a Christ follower is actually realizing the need for a Savior and the admittance that we are sinners needing redemption. Our pride (from satan) doesn't want us to realize, or admit, we need saving!

Let's move onto the 'B' in the ABC's of salvation. 'B' stands for believing in your heart that Jesus is Lord. To quote Romans again, 10:9-10, Paul states, "if you confess with your mouth that Jesus is Lord and believe in your heart that God raised Him from the dead, you will be saved." If you are not at all familiar with scripture, believing may be a challenge. Here is where the Holy Spirit works in a person's heart.

The 'C' in the ABCs of salvation stands for call. This is the part where you call upon the name of the Lord to be saved! Romans 10:13 states, "For everyone who calls on the name of the Lord will be saved." This is when you can claim Christ's victory over sin and death. Because of the blood of Christ, we are made new. God does not hold our sins against us. When God looks upon the saved believer, He sees His perfect son, Christ. We are made righteous because Jesus was obedient to take the wrath of our sins, past, present, and future. He was and is victorious over sin!

If you have chosen to follow Christ after reading this story, or if you have become interested in learning more, I would love to chat with you. Being a follower of Jesus Christ is a little bit like a marathon, and the end is either leaving this earth through death, or taken to be with Christ during the rapture.

The rapture is when Jesus Christ calls all redeemed believers in Him to heaven before the Seven Year Tribulation. Let's find scripture that is so encouraging, knowing we will meet Jesus in the air before the Tribulation begins. In Paul's letter to the Thessalonicans, he was assuring them that they didn't miss the rapture. Also, Paul was answering their question of "what happened to the Christians who die before He comes?" Paul's answer in 1 Thessalonians 4:13 states, "But we do not want you to be uninformed, brothers, about those who are asleep, that you may not grieve as others do who have no hope. For since we believe that Jesus died and rose again, even so, through Jesus, God will bring with Him those who have fallen asleep. For this we declare to you by a word from the Lord, that we who are alive, who are left until the coming of the Lord, will not precede those who have fallen asleep. For the Lord Himself will descend from heaven with a cry of command, with the voice of an archangel, and with the sound of the trumpet of God. And the dead in Christ will rise first. Then we who are alive, who are left, will be caught up together with them in the clouds to meet the Lord in the air, and so we will always be with the Lord. Therefore encourage one another with these words."

In Paul's letter to Titus, he states, "For the grace of God has appeared, bringing salvation for all people, training us to renounce ungodliness and worldly passions, and to live self-controlled upright, and godly lives in the present age, waiting for our BLESSED HOPE, the appearing of the glory of our great God and Savior Jesus Christ." Titus 2:11-13

While we wait to either be raptured (when Jesus calls the redeemed believers home, before the Tribulation), or ruptured (death on this earth), we are to strive to be like Christ, sanctified and holy. The whole point of salvation is to conform to Christ's likeness. This can only be done by being in His Word and abiding in Christ. I love this blog that Kayla wrote about her Bible.

Mark it Up!
(blog by Kayla, February 2014)

"I don't know about you, but...I write in my Bible.
A lot.
I mark it up.
Maybe it's simply because I love annotating and post-it notes, and highlighters and journals and gel pens.

Maybe not.

God gave his word to US to devour and share and hide in our hearts. How incredibly blessed we are with this gift?!

We need to SOAK IT UP.

We need to make it personal.

"A bible that's falling apart usually belongs to someone who isn't." Charles Spurgeon

Our Bibles can't stay on our nightstands collecting dust. I realized how important making our Bibles personal when I left my Bible at church on Sunday. I could have borrowed a Bible or used one of numerous others lying around my room and house, but there is something about the Bible we use on a consistent basis that helps us dive into the Word with a profound eagerness. In my Bible I've written prayers, scrawled in the margins, asked questions and made comments. It's practically a journal.

I'm resolving, TODAY, that I'm gonna be in the word more, because frankly, I haven't been too appreciative lately of the fact that God gave it to ME to use! I look to everything else except what's right in front of me, readily available. Aside from giving Himself to me Jesus has given me the truest form of wisdom to be found.

'...he rewards those who earnestly seek Him.' Hebrews 11:6

Will you resolve to seek Him as well? Kayla"

be glad
like the prophets
who were persecuted
stay salty
matt 5:13

shine your
for others

a city on a hill
cannot be hidden

DO NOT
Hide
YOUR light
AND
Waste the
GIFT it is...

8 "Blessed are the pure in heart, for they shall see God.

9 "Blessed are the peacemakers, for they shall be called sons[1] of God.

10 "Blessed are those who are persecuted for righteousness' sake, for theirs is the kingdom of heaven.

11 "Blessed are you when others revile you and persecute you and utter all kinds of evil against you falsely on my account. 12 Rejoice and be glad, for your reward is great in heaven, for so they persecuted the prophets who were before you.

Salt and Light

13 "You are the salt of the earth, but if salt has lost its taste, how shall its saltiness be restored? It is no longer good for anything except to be thrown out and trampled under people's feet. 14 "You are the light of the world. A city set on a hill cannot be hidden. 15 Nor do people light a lamp and put it under a basket, but on a stand, and it gives light to all in the house. 16 In the same way, let your light shine before others, so that[2] they may see your good works and give glory to your Father who is in heaven.

Christ Came to Fulfill the Law

17 "Do not think that I have come to abolish the Law or the Prophets; I have not come to abolish them but to fulfill them. 18 For truly, I say to you, until heaven and earth pass away, not an iota, not a dot, will pass from the Law until all is accomplished. 19 Therefore whoever relaxes one of the least of these commandments and teaches others to do the same will be called least in the kingdom of heaven, but whoever does them and teaches them will be called great in the kingdom of heaven. 20 For I tell you, unless your righteousness exceeds that of the scribes and Pharisees, you will never enter the kingdom of heaven.

Anger

21 "You have heard that it was said to those of old, [a] 'You shall not murder; and whoever murders will be liable to judgment.' 22 But I say to you that everyone who is angry with his brother[3] will be liable to judgment; whoever insults[4] his brother will be liable to the council; and whoever says, 'You fool!' will be liable to the hell[5] of fire. 23 So if you are offering your gift at the altar and there remember that your brother

there before the altar and
to your brother, and then
gift. 25 Come to terms qui
while you are going with
accuser hand you over
judge to the guard, and
26 Truly, I say to you,
you have paid the last p

Lust

27 "You have heard tha
not commit adultery.'
everyone who looks at
intent has already com
her in his heart. 29 If your
sin, tear it out and thro
that you lose one of yo
your whole body be thr
your right hand causes
throw it away. For it is
of your members than
go into hell.

Divorce

31 "It was also said,
wife, let him give her
32 But I say to you that
his wife, except on the g
rality, makes her comm
marries a divorced wor

Oaths

33 "Again you have h
those of old, 'You sha
shall perform to the Lor
34 But I say to you, Do
either by heaven, for
35 or by the earth, for
Jerusalem, for it is the
36 And do not take an oa
cannot make one hair w
you say be simply 'Yes'
than this comes from

Retaliation

38 "You have heard t
for an eye and a tooth
to you, Do not resist t
'if anyone slaps you on
him the other also. 40 A
you and take your tu

[1] Greek huioi; see Preface [2] Or house [3a] Let your light so shine before others that [3] Some manuscripts insert without cause [4] Greek says
also verses 29, 30 [5] Greek kodrantes, Roman copper coin (Latin quadrans...

now, but I will see you again, and your hearts will rejoice, and no one will take your joy from you. ²²In that day you will ask nothing of me. Truly, truly, I say to you, whatever you ask of the Father in my name, he will give it to you. ²⁴Until now you have asked nothing in my name. Ask, and you will receive, that your joy may be full.

I Have Overcome the World

²⁵"I have said these things to you in figures of speech. The hour is coming when I will no longer speak to you in figures of speech but will tell you plainly about the Father. ²⁶In that day you will ask in my name, and I do not say to you that I will ask the Father on your behalf, ²⁷for the Father himself loves you, because you have loved me and have believed that I came from God.¹ ²⁸I came from the Father and have come into the world, and now I am leaving the world and going to the Father."

²⁹His disciples said, "Ah, now you are speaking plainly and not using figurative speech! ³⁰Now we know that you know all things and do not need anyone to question you; this is why we believe that you came from God." ³¹Jesus answered them, "Do you now believe? ³²Behold, the hour is coming, indeed it has come, when you will be scattered, each to his own home, and will leave me alone. Yet I am not alone, for the Father is with me. ³³I have said these things to you, that in me you may have peace. In the world you will have tribulation. But take heart; I have overcome the world."

The High Priestly Prayer

7 When Jesus had spoken these words, he lifted up his eyes to heaven, and said, "Father, the hour has come; glorify your Son that the Son may glorify you, ²since you have given him authority over all flesh, to give eternal life to all whom you have given him. ³And this is eternal life, that they know you the only true God, and Jesus Christ whom you have sent. ⁴I glorified you on earth, having accomplished the work that you gave me to do. ⁵And now, Father, glorify me in your own presence with the glory that I had with you before the world existed.

⁶"I have manifested your name to the people whom you gave me out of the world. Yours they were, and you gave them to me, and they have

thing that you have given me is from you. ⁸For I have given them the words that you gave me, and they have received them and have come to know in truth that I came from you; and they have believed that you sent me. ⁹I am praying for them. I am not praying for the world but for those whom you have given me, for they are yours. ¹⁰All mine are yours, and yours are mine, and I am glorified in them. ¹¹And I am no longer in the world, but they are in the world, and I am coming to you. Holy Father, keep them in your name, which you have given me, that they may be one, even as we are one. ¹²While I was with them, I kept them in your name, which you have given me. I have guarded them, and not one of them has been lost except the son of destruction,² that the Scripture might be fulfilled. ¹³But now I am coming to you, and these things I speak in the world, that they may have my joy fulfilled in themselves. ¹⁴I have given them your word, and the world has hated them because they are not of the world, just as I am not of the world. ¹⁵I do not ask that you take them out of the world, but that you keep them from the evil one.³ ¹⁶They are not of the world, just as I am not of the world. ¹⁷Sanctify them⁴ in the truth; your word is truth. ¹⁸As you sent me into the world, so I have sent them into the world. ¹⁹And for their sake I consecrate myself,⁴ that they also may be sanctified⁴ in truth.

²⁰"I do not ask for these only, but also for those who will believe in me through their word, ²¹that they may all be one, just as you, Father, are in me, and I in you, that they also may be in us, so that the world may believe that you have sent me. ²²The glory that you have given me I have given to them, that they may be one even as we are one, ²³I in them and you in me, that they may become perfectly one, so that the world may know that you sent me and loved them even as you loved me. ²⁴Father, I desire that they also, whom you have given me, may be with me where I am, to see my glory that you have given me because you loved me before the foundation of the world. ²⁵O righteous Father, even though the world does not know you, I know you, and these know that you have sent me. ²⁶I made known to them your name, and I will continue to make it known, that the love with which you have loved me may be in them, and I in them."

¹ Some manuscripts from the Father ² Or from evil ³ Greek Set them apart (for holy service to God) ⁴ Or I sanctify myself or I set myself apart (for holy service to God) ⁵ Greek set apart for holy service to God

Being a follower of Christ is a lifelong journey, and it's also a narrow path. Matthew 7:13 says, "Enter by the narrow gate. For the gate is wide and the way is easy that leads to destruction, and those who enter by it are many. For the gate is narrow and the way is hard that leads to life, and those who find it are few." There are times when it is easier, when you are in a good place in life. I find that those are the times I'm actually further from the Lord. I get busy with life and kids, things are going smoothly, so I don't feel the urgency to be in Scripture. If you are a new believer, a mature believer, or a future believer, make it a discipline to be in the Word and pray. I urge you to consider the gift it is to have God's Word available to us to help us live like Christ until we meet Him.

1 John 5:13 states, "I write these things to you who believe in the name of the Son of God, that you may know that you have eternal life." This blows my mind that we can receive this FREE gift just by acknowledging Him as our Lord. We don't have to work and do good deeds in order to gain access to heaven. In fact, this would be adding to the gospel. We are to be obedient when God places someone in our life who needs the gospel or who needs material things. But, if that becomes a focus (good works), you have lost sight of the fact that God already did the work by shedding his blood on the cross.

Before I end our story, I'd like to share with you this blog post from Kayla. I know that in her life she shared the gospel with others, whether through words or actions, or just being a friend to someone. Here is a blog post that breaks down the gospel in her own sweet words. The fact that she understood it so clearly from such a young age is a testament to her spirituality.

When Everything Is Crashing Down
(blog by Kayla, April 2013)

"I've been thinking. A lot. As I watch our country fall apart, I look around and search for the faith our country was built on. A few favorite quotes come to mind.

'If we ever forget that we are one nation under God, then we will be a nation gone under'—Ronald Reagan

'God allows in his wisdom what he could prevent by his power'– Graham Cooke

'When you reach the end of your rope, tie a knot and hang on'—Thomas Jefferson

There is so much truth in these words.

These days, I cannot say anything on social media about God without getting a bunch of feedback. Mostly negative, from both my Christian and non-Christian friends. For a long while, I sat back, shut my mouth, and ignored things I felt were 'controversial.' Over time, I learned that just because I shut up no one else would. You're either for something or against it. Christians shouldn't be silent, but no one should be hateful.

99.999999% of the few debates I either indirectly or directly become involved in, don't go so hot. 99.9999999% of what I am trying to say doesn't exactly come out how I intended. By the time it comes out my readers or listeners are crawling all over me. The latest accusation from an 'acquaintance' who is a self-proclaimed atheist was in regards to all that happened over the country last week. He wanted a factual response. Some believers I know are great at proving things with bits and pieces of science and whatnot. I on the other hand am not. **God created us to be with Him.**

Let me just make this clear. AGAIN. I'm writing this because I care. I have such a huge treasure. One that I can share over and over and over again! We're not all that we knock ourselves to be. **Our sins separate us from God.** That SHOULD be obvious by now. But thousands of years later, let's face it, we aren't doing so well at learning from our mistakes. When I say 'we' I mean 'me' and 'you'. I'm not trying to exclude myself. God wiped out sin, but he ALLOWED it back into the world after he gave us a glorious second chance. God forgives all sins "70 X 7" times. He gave us what we wanted. Free will. Sin was our choice. Of course God didn't leave us destined for hell as we deserved. On the contrary he provided the ultimate sacrifice. More is never enough for us. Those who choose the gift of life he gives us are saved from judgement forever. Or we can shove it back in God's face. At this point in the convo I'm typically cut off, so thanks for reading on. I don't have to sit home with a checklist of things to do because I'm not going to get it all right. Without Jesus, I would never be able to live up to standards outlined in the Bible. **Sins cannot be removed by good deeds.**

"But what about the Old Testament? It says there... We don't stone people, We don't eat crawfish, people made animal sacrifices"........the list goes on and on and on. My small group discussed this whole OT 'So what?' question. So "what about it?"

In the Old Testament these 'rules and regulations' were made because believers didn't have any other choice. Let me elaborate. Jesus hadn't come yet. Jesus is the Ultimate Sacrifice *who paid the price of our sins. Mine, yours multiplied by every-one on this planet. He bore the weight of it all.* **Paying the price for sin Jesus died and rose again.** *All those things were their SECOND CHANCE which, in the New Testament is Jesus. If you're still with me, can we just revel in the fact that we, as undeserving as we are, can have what nobody else has.* **Everyone who trusts in Him has eternal life.** *The gift that supersedes all riches.*

I'm not going to 'act' smart and pretend I know why every-thing happened in Boston, MA and Waco, TX. I'm not in any way trying to justify anything saying God does whatever it takes to be near us. Is Jesus dying on the cross not enough evidence or proof that he loves us? Rest in the knowledge that no matter how bad we screw up, he will keep on forgiving us. Again, and again, and again, and again, and again, and again, and again, and again, and again......I think you get the picture.

In my college bible study 'Ignite' today-it was my first time—a fellow believer from Egypt, said something quite profound. Something that believers have to constantly remind themselves. He said with a strong accent, "I have three citi-zen-ships. Egypt, America, and Heaven." How cool is that?!

Life with Jesus starts now and lasts forever.
G.O.S.P.E.L—The Greatest Story Ever Told. *Kayla"*

As I end in what seems like just a glimpse into our story, I want to acknowledge that writing is hard! As I've worked on telling this story, there are times when I have no idea what to write about, what to include, what to delete. I worry that the flow of it isn't written well, or that the reader will be confused going back and forth in time. For the last post, I will include how Kayla felt about writing... which I now understand so much better and which helps me to feel closer to her.

Writing is Hard
(blog by Kayla, March 2014)

"Every writer has this defining point in their writing journey where they ask themselves the questions: "Why am I writing?" "Is it all worth it?" "Who should I write for?" "Should I write for high stats, or what's on my heart?"

I've been blogging for a year. I haven't even reached 2,000 views. I'm pretty sure I get the most views when my mom shares my posts on her Facebook page. My fan-base is limited. (I'm not sure it even qualifies as a fan-base). I've signed up for about every suggested social media site one could think of. And, consequently, I haven't seen much change in my stats.

I continue writing. If I don't write, I feel as if part of me is missing. Still, it'd be nice for a complete stranger who is more successful than I have been to recognize my work. There is no denying that wishful thinking.

I hate sounding cliche, but no great thing comes easily. Good things come with hours, weeks, even years of hard work. That's what I missed when I first began my journey. I missed the tears, the calloused fingers, the rejections, the failed attempts. The ceremonious burning of drafts. The promise to get up, leave, and never write another word. Those are defining moments in any artist's life. The rise to fame hardly compares to the time spent laboring to arrive at that point.

> *So if it's not easy, why do it? I'll tell you why. Because that one person who is impacted by your writing, makes up for the lack of viewers, the low stats, the rejection letters.*
>
> *One of my Twitter followers responded to my post stepping away for awhile with these words: "You shine." Folks, that's why I keep writing.*
>
> *If you write for numbers, there's a good chance you might not write anything great at all. Keep at it. Kayla"*

My hope in writing this story was to share the gift of Kayla. The gift that was clearly sent to us from God. And while her life on this Earth was short, it was a beacon of light that shined on all who were graced with the gift of knowing her. And although she is no longer here on this Earth, she has left us her words of Hope. I pray that when you close this book, you can have Hope. That is what Kayla wanted for herself and for others. May you live with HOPE until we are all together with the Lord. And don't forget to share your story! God bless you.

Oh—in case you were wondering—we are blessed that Charley is still with our family.

Made in the USA
Coppell, TX
17 April 2022

76711733R00095